Office Soft Skills

Working with North Americans

Joan Bartel

WAYZGOOSE PRESS

Office Soft Skills: Working with North Americans
Copyright © 2018 by Wayzgoose Press

Third Edition

ISBN-13: 978-1-938757-39-6

Edited by Maggie Sokolik
Book Design by DJ Rogers Design
Illustrations by David Meredith
Published in the United States by Wayzgoose Press

Endorsements

The material in *Office Soft Skills* is definite "need-to-know" content for ESL students preparing to enter the workforce. I use it in my class to teach workplace preparation, and the students eagerly engage with the topic and activities.

Gwen Zeldenrust
Occupation Specific Language Teacher
Mohawk College, Hamilton, Canada

∽

Joan's book is a must-read for any job seeker. The numerous examples of workplace scenarios are required reading for those unfamiliar with North American workplace culture.
A great read - a superior resource.

Michelle Edmunds
Founder, FOCUSINDUSTRY

∽

I highly recommend *Office Soft Skills* to anyone new to the business culture in North America. I gave this book to a staff member whose only American cultural experience was as a college student. He loved the book, and his business credibility grew as he put the lessons into practice.

J. Rodriguez
Technical Manager, California

∽

The term "North America" in this book means the northern part of the continent, namely Canada and the

United States of America, and refers primarily to the English-speaking population.

∽

This book is dedicated to the internationally trained professionals who immigrated to Toronto and briefly became my students during their first years in Canada.

Table of Contents

PART 1

SOFT SKILLS FOR MAKING A GOOD FIRST IMPRESSION

UNIT 1
INTRODUCTIONS IN PERSON

In this unit you can test your skills in face-to-face introductions. You will find answers to questions like:

- Do you know how to introduce a colleague to your boss? What do you say? Who starts?

- What does your handshake say about you?

You will also read about air-kisses and hugs – and when they are appropriate.

 Key words: *etiquette, network, introduce, gender-neutral, handshake, extend your hand, firm, discrimination*

There are 8 questions and 16 points in this unit.

1

Do you know the basic etiquette of introductions?

1. SITUATION: Waiting for a huge company meeting to start, you see a woman from a branch office who is an expert in your field. You want to meet her.

QUESTION: Is it OK to introduce yourself to her?

☐ **a.** It isn't polite to introduce yourself to someone who isn't expecting it, especially if you have a lower job or social position.

☐ **b.** It depends on gender:
If you are a woman, you can go to her and introduce yourself.
If you are a man, you can't introduce yourself to her. You should wait for an opportunity when *she* can begin the introduction.

☐ **c.** If you have something to say or ask, you can go to her and introduce yourself. Anyone can introduce her-/himself to others at a meeting.

2. When you are introducing two men to each other, whose name do you say first?

☐ **a.** The senior person's name, for example:
"Boris Senior, I'd like you to meet Mario Junior."

☐ **b.** The junior person's name, for example:
"Mario Junior, I'd like you to meet Boris Senior."

☐ **c.** It doesn't matter. There are no rules about this in North America.

3. When you are introduced to someone, who should extend his/her hand first? [Choose as many answers as necessary.]

☐ **a.** a woman to a man

☐ **b.** a man to a woman

☐ **c.** a senior person to a junior person

☐ **d.** a junior person to a senior person

☐ **e.** It doesn't matter. There are no rules about this in North America.

4. At an introduction, if someone doesn't want to shake hands:

☐ **a.** That's OK. North Americans allow all kinds of behaviors.

☐ **b.** It's OK if the person is a woman because women don't shake hands as much as men do.

☐ **c.** People might feel that that behavior is rude or even insulting – unless a reason is given.

☐ **d.** If that person's usual custom is to kiss people lightly on both cheeks instead of shaking hands, it's not a problem in North America.

5. Your handshake makes an impression. Does it reflect your leadership skills? Many hiring mangers think:

☐ **a.** if you *squeeze* the other person's hand, it means you are a strong leader.

☐ **b.** if you have a weak handshake, it means you are shy or not a strong leader.

☐ **c.** both a and b.

☐ **d.** your handshake doesn't reflect your personality or leadership skills.

6. SITUATION: You are at a job interview. After introductions, the conversation continues.

QUESTION: What is a common topic of conversation at the beginning of an interview? (More than one answer might be correct, but choose just one.)

☐ **a.** Families

☐ **b.** Where you were born

☐ **c.** Your health and ability to work

☐ **d.** Transportation: how you got to the interview

7. How often do North Americans shake hands with their office colleagues?

☐ **a.** Only once, at the introduction.

☐ **b.** Once a day when everybody arrives at the office.

☐ **c.** Twice a day, at the beginning and end of the day.

8. SITUATION: You want to make a good impression when you meet new people at a meeting, new job or interview. A first impression is based on more than clothes.

QUESTION: Which of the following is <u>not</u> part of making a good first impression in North America?

☐ **a.** a smile

☐ **b.** perfume

☐ **c.** feeling confident

☐ **d.** posture (standing straight)

☐ **e.** hair (style and cleanliness)

UNIT 1. ANSWERS:

2 points for 1c, 2a, 3c, 3e, 4c, 5b, 6d, 7a, 8b
1 point for 4a, 5c. **And ½ point** for 2c.
If you scored 14 points, you know more about
introductions than many Canadians and Americans!

□ ←   ←   ← WRITE YOUR SCORE HERE.

1. a [0 points]: **Meetings and conferences are, in fact, a very good place to meet people.** The purpose of a conference is to network (meet people in your field) as well as to learn new things and ideas. Introduce yourself to as many people as you want!

1. b [0 points]: **Men and women are equal** in the U.S. and Canada and introductions are gender-neutral. Either a man or a woman can begin an introduction.

1. c [2 points]: **You can go to her and introduce yourself** no matter whether you are a man or a woman. There are no restrictive rules about this.

2. a [2 points]: **The senior person's name is first.** For example: "Mr. Senior, I'd like you to meet Mr. Junior." That is a rule. It doesn't matter whether the senior person is a man or a woman, so the same rules apply for women – but see **2. c** below.

2. b [0 points]: Wrong answer.

HANDSHAKES: WHO AND WHEN

2. c [½ point]: There is a rule: see **2. a** above. However, **not everybody knows** and follows this etiquette (so you get a ½ point). Don't feel insulted if you are introduced differently from the proper way.

3. a, b, d [0 points]: Wrong answer.

3. c or e [2 points]: Traditionally, the senior person should extend his/her hand first. (Follow this etiquette in a job interview.) **Nowadays, it doesn't matter** very much; the etiquette rules have relaxed.

4. a [1 point]: While North American culture is generally liberal, **many people think it's not appropriate to refuse to shake someone's hand.** They will feel uncomfortable because, in North American culture, the only traditional reason for not shaking hands is distrust or extreme dislike. On the one side: Of course, you have a right to refuse to shake hands, for example, if your religion forbids it. And you are being considerate if you don't offer your hand because you have a cold. A one-sentence **explanation** for your refusal is helpful and a good idea. On the other side: If you are introduced to someone who doesn't want to shake your hand, a polite reaction is to smile and say *"That's OK"* and accept their preference.

4. b [0 points]: See #**3. e** above. There is no gender difference in hand-shaking rules in North America.

4. c [2 points]: Among people with no multi-cultural experience, that behavior can be seen as rude. But see **4. a** above about giving a reason to ease the situation.

11

KISSING AT INTRODUCTIONS

4. d [0 points] **Kissing at introductions**: Some cultural groups of people, like movie stars or some people from South American or Middle Eastern origins, have a custom of kissing one or both cheeks very lightly instead of shaking hands. One-cheek kisses are more common among English-speakers in Canada, and a person's lips do not actually touch the other's skin; this is called an "air-kiss." People in the province of Quebec (and from some other cultures) might touch both cheeks with two or more kisses.

But not everyone feels comfortable with such closeness, especially in an office setting. Canadians don't usually touch each other at work. If you try to air-kiss or hug someone who doesn't want to, that may be called harassment.

If you want to kiss at an introduction, watch the other person: if he/she extends a hand, it is a sign that he/she would rather shake than kiss. You should respect that wish and shake hands.

If you don't want to kiss or hug during an introduction, you can offer your hand for a handshake instead.

Note: In informal or large group situations, like a party or in a meeting, sometimes *nobody* shakes hands; other times, *everybody* shakes hands or gives air kisses as greetings. That's OK if everybody acts in the same way.

FIRM AND SOFT HANDSHAKES

5. a [0 points]: **The squeeze handshake** does <u>not</u> represent strong leadership skills, according to a survey among hiring managers.[1] Squeezing is too strong to be polite and can hurt. If someone squeezes your hand hard, he/she is usually a domineering person who wants to control the situation. This person might want to lead but only in his/her own way, without regard for other people's feelings or points of view. Therefore, the squeezer isn't usually considered to be a good leader or team member.

5. b [2 points]: **A weak handshake = you are shy or not a strong leader.** A weak handshake, also called a "limp noodle" or "dead fish" shake, doesn't make a good first impression in most of North America. Men and women with a weak handshake are usually considered to be weak in leadership, teamwork skills, general energy, and enthusiasm. In fact, recent research showed a direct match between a handshake at an interview and a job offer afterwards: a strong (firm) handshake was a characteristic of a strong candidate for a job, while a weak handshake was a characteristic of a weak candidate.[2] Note: A strong handshake is not the same as a squeeze handshake.

5. c [1 point]; **5. d** [0 points].

Cultural Note: Handshakes

In contrast to the majority North American custom, a soft handshake is actually preferred among First Nations peoples in Canada and Native Americans in the Southwest of the United States.

13

JOB INTERVIEWS

6. a, b, c [0 points]: **It is illegal** in the U.S. and Canada for an interviewer to ask about family status, country of origin, personal health, or disability. It is also illegal to ask about age or religion. All of these questions could possibly lead to discrimination against some people. The interviewer can only ask whether the candidate has any issues that would prevent him/her from doing the duties of the job.

6. d [2 points]: **After introductions**, interviewers often ask "Did you have any trouble finding us?" or say "I hope you didn't have to travel too far to get here." They don't expect a long answer. The question is just an easy question to start. Its purpose is to relax everybody with friendly, everyday conversation. After that, the serious interview begins, with questions about experience and qualifications, etc.

Job Tip: Likability

Besides handshakes, other factors are also decisive in a hiring decision. A Harvard Business Review report about hiring states that managers tend to hire people whom they like (who are likable people). The manager thinks the candidate will get along well with company teams and can imagine working well with the candidate.[3] In fact, several studies and surveys have shown that likability is as important as technical skills and knowledge for getting a job and getting ahead.

INTRODUCTIONS AND HANDSHAKES AT THE OFFICE

> *True story*: On his first day at work, an immigrant from South Asia was introduced to everybody. When he met his boss, an older woman, he said with a friendly smile, "Oh, you must be a grandmother!" In his culture that is a compliment – but not in North America, where it's taboo to suggest that anyone looks old. After a moment of speechlessness, his boss responded politely, "No, not yet. But some day, I hope."

New employees: In some companies, a new employee won't be introduced to everyone on the first day. Instead, the supervisor or manager introduces the new person to only one or two staff members, shows him/her where to sit and hands out a company policy manual. Then he/she is left alone to read it and work. Sometimes new staff are not even told the locations of restrooms and the lunch room!

If this happens to you, you should introduce yourself to office staff around you whenever you see them. You might find that some people are very willing to talk with you, while others are "too busy" to respond.

> **Job Tip:** The office or company receptionist can be a good source of advice and help, so when you start a new job, be sure to introduce yourself to her (the receptionist is almost always a woman) and learn her name.

7. a [2 points]: You shake hands with colleagues in your office only once, at the introduction, not every day. (You might shake again after a long absence.)

7. b and c [0 points]: Shaking hands with coworkers every day isn't the custom in most of North America.

FIRST IMPRESSIONS ARE ALSO BASED ON:

8. a [0 points]: A **smile** is very important in North American culture! A smile shows that you want to get along, have good relationships. In the business world, it may be more common among women than men, and among lower-level employees than executives. But if you don't smile sometimes, coworkers (and job interviewers) might think you are unfriendly.

8. b [2 points]: **Perfume** is favored by women in many countries but not often by people at work in Canada or the United States. About 40% of workplaces are now "scent-free." That means that employees are asked not to wear perfumes or scents.[4] The reason is that some people have allergies or sensitivities to smells like perfume (or cigarette smoke).

8. c, d [0 points]: **When you feel confident, you walk straighter** (and have good eye contact). Your good body language makes a positive impression – see the woman on the right on page 6. If you have confidence in your abilities, others will have confidence in you, too.

8. e [0 points]: **Hair** (style and cleanliness) is part of a first impression. In business and politics, and particularly for women CEOs and politicians, hairstyles are part of image – and sometimes make the news.[5]

> **Tip: Poor grooming (clean hair and body) and inappropriate clothing** choices really annoy interviewers: most hirers say they dislike badly dressed candidates. For professional and office job applicants, a suit or blazer with pants/skirt are usually good choices – the higher the position, the more formal the clothing. If you aren't sure what to wear, it is better to overdress than underdress.

Business dress: 4 traditional levels of formality

Formal corporate:
A dark suit or three-piece suit (suit with a vest), with a tie for men, and dark leather shoes. Women's suits may have pants or a skirt. This is conservative business clothing for men and women in law and a few other professions.

Business:
A suit (with pants or skirt for women), and for men a tie. In some workplaces, women's skirts may not be short. Lighter suit colors are acceptable in warm weather but sandals are not. Women may wear some jewelry. Non-western clothing, such as a sari or turban, is a non-traditional option in some companies.

Business casual:
For men: a shirt with collar, with or without a tie (only about 5 percent of men wear ties at work[6]) and pants. For women: a shirt or blouse with sleeves, with a skirt or pants. For all: a jacket or blazer is nice but optional; a sweater or cardigan is also fine. Non-western or ethnic clothing of similar formality is often OK. In some companies, clean, well-fitting jeans and dressy sandals are allowed.

Casual:
Office clothing: A shirt or blouse (sleeveless is OK for women) with pants or jeans – or with a skirt, long shorts or capri pants for women. Some companies may allow sandals and T-shirts without logos or words (slogans). Non-western or ethnic clothing is also fine. However, sports and weekend clothes, for example, flip-flops, sweatshirts, hoodies, running suits, and short shorts are usually not allowed in the office.

HOW TO SAY IT: INTRODUCTIONS

a) Sample self-introduction at a conference or meeting

"Mr. Park? I've heard a lot about your work on the ZYX Project. I'd like to introduce myself. My name's _____ and I've been involved in a similar project in my branch."

Think of a place where you could practice self-introductions and go there to try it several times.

b) Sample introductions of a new employee

1. Formal introduction
M = Manager, who makes the introduction
C = Company President Daniel Senior
N = New manager Maria Junior

M: *Mr. Senior, may I introduce you to our new Manager, Maria Junior?*

C: *How do you do, Maria. Welcome to the company.*

M: *Maria, this is our CEO, Mr. Senior [or Daniel Senior].*

N: *How do you do, Mr. Senior. I'm glad to be here.*

Note: The proper response to *How do you do?* is *How do you do?* It isn't a question, but rather a formal statement that is part of a formal introduction. What is the equivalent informal statement? See the next page.

2. Semi-formal introduction
H = HR Manager, who makes the introduction
M = Manager Anita Ford
E = new employee Edward (Ed) Lee

H: *Anita, let me introduce you to our new staff
member, Ed Lee. Ed, this is Anita Ford,
Transportation Manager.*

M: *Nice to meet you, Ed. Welcome to the company.*

E: *Nice to meet you, too, Ms. Ford. Glad to be here.*

M: *Please call me 'Anita.'*

E: *Sure, Anita.*

3. Informal introduction
M = Manager/Supervisor, who makes the introduction
S = Staff member Sue Zhou
E = new employee Edward (Ed) Lee

M: *Sue, this is your new team member, Ed Lee. Ed,
you'll be working with Sue here.*
(Or: *Ed, come over here, please, and meet Sue Zhou.
You'll be working on her team.*)

S: *Oh, hi, Ed. Nice to meet you. Great to have you
on the team.*

E: *Nice to meet you, too, Sue. Glad to be here.
What's your current project?*

ACTION: Find an association or community group
with your interests. Go to a meeting, introduce yourself.
In class: Practice introducing classmates to each other.

UNIT 2
MAKING A GOOD FIRST IMPRESSION
ON THE PHONE

In this unit you can show your knowledge of phone etiquette. You will find answers to questions like:

- What are some general rules about polite business phone calls?

- When is texting better than calling?

- What should you say in your office voicemail greeting?

 Key words: *smartphone, answering the phone, customer service, texting, voicemail greeting, follow-up call, multitasking*

There are 8 questions and 16 points in this unit.

1. Is it ever OK to talk on your cell when other people are around you? In most places in the list below, it is *not* acceptable (except maybe in a real emergency).

Which place is **OK**? (Choose the best answer.)

☐ **a.** at a restaurant with colleagues

☐ **b.** in a business meeting

☐ **c.** in a college or university lecture/class

☐ **d.** in the office restroom

☐ **e.** in a bus or train

2. SITUATION: Bookkeeper Elena Clinton is sitting at her desk at Giganticorp in Mississauga. Her phone rings. She doesn't have Call Display on her phone so she doesn't know who is calling.

QUESTION: How should she answer the phone? What should she say? Choose the most appropriate response.

☐ **a.** "Hello."

☐ **b.** "Giganticorp."

☐ **c.** "Clinton."

☐ **d.** "I am Elena Clinton. Good morning."

☐ **e.** "Elena Clinton, Bookkeeping Department."

3. Companies expect their employees to be polite and helpful on the phone. Nobody likes talking to an employee who is rude or unhelpful.

SITUATION: You are talking to an client or customer on the phone. He/She is beginning to get angry and asks for a special service that is against company policy.

QUESTION: What should you say? Choose the best response.

☐ **a.** *"No."*

☐ **b.** *"Oh, that's a problem. I can't do that."*

☐ **c.** *"I'm afraid that's not possible."*

☐ **b.** *"I'll ask my manager about that."*

4. Which is the method of communication that most executives (high-level bosses) **prefer for messages from staff?**

☐ **a.** an email

☐ **b.** a face-to-face meeting

☐ **c.** a memo on paper

☐ **d.** a phone call or phone message

5. Smartphones allow both texting and speaking.

QUESTION: In what business situations is it best to send a text, and when is it better to speak to the person you are trying to reach?

a. Texting is better: _____

_____

_____

_____

_____

b. Speaking on the phone is better: _____

_____

_____

_____

_____

Note: Your answer might reflect your age!

6. SITUATION: In your voicemail greeting at work, you say your name and a brief message.

QUESTION: Which of the following is NOT an appropriate message?

☐ **a.** I am away this afternoon at a doctor's appointment. Please leave me a message, and I'll get back to you when I feel better.

☐ **b.** I am either away from my desk or on another line. Please leave me a message, and I'll get back to you as soon as possible.

☐ **c.** I am not at my desk today, April 11th, until four p.m. Please leave me a message, and I'll get back to you at the end of the day.

☐ **d.** I am on a business trip until April 11th. Please leave a message. My colleague Hugo will pick up my calls and get back to you.

☐ **e.** All of the above are appropriate.

7. SITUATION: You try to contact a colleague or client by phone but the person isn't available and didn't leave a detailed voicemail greeting, so you leave a message. (It isn't an emergency situation.)

QUESTION: If you don't get a call back soon, how long should you wait before you call again?

☐ **a.** You should not call back again. Calling more than once is bad manners.

☐ **b.** one hour

☐ **c.** 2-3 hours

☐ **d.** one day

☐ **e.** 2-3 days

8. Nowadays many people are used to working and playing with technological devices.

True or False? We can manage multitasking efficiently, for example, talk on the phone while browsing the Web and/or reading a memo.

☐ **a.** False – Multitasking is less efficient than doing one task at a time.

☐ **b.** True – People can multitask efficiently.

☐ **c.** True – People can manage multitasking, but only with simple, mechanical tasks like photocopying or casual activities like chatting.

True story: *An investment advisor and his colleagues, when having a business lunch meeting, put their smart phones in the middle of the table. The first person who reaches for a phone during lunch has to pay the bill for the whole group.*

UNIT 2. ANSWERS:

Two points for 1e, 2e, 3c, 4a, 6a, 7d, 8c
½ point for 1a, 1b, 3d, 8a, 8b
For question #5: See page 35.

□   ← ← ←   WRITE YOUR SCORE HERE.

1. a [½ point]: Talking on a cell phone at a restaurant: When you are with business colleagues or clients, it is good manners to give them your full attention. If you leave your cell on, and answer it if it rings, that implies that the people you are currently talking with are not important. It doesn't make a good impression. It is bad manners – even though many people do it.

An exception [for the ½ point]: If you know that a very important call might come soon, let your colleagues know that *before* it comes. Then excuse yourself and move away from the group if your call comes and keep your phone conversation as short and quiet as possible.

1. b [½ point]: Talking on a phone during a meeting: No, this isn't good etiquette…but many people admit that they do it in some meetings. (More about meeting etiquette in UNIT 6.)

1. c [0 points]: Talking on a phone during class: It is rude to let your cell phone ring in a class, as well as in a movie, concert, etc. The ringing sound/music distracts other listeners. And your conversation, even if you are walking out of the room, is annoying too.

WHERE NOT TO TALK ON THE PHONE

1. c (continued): In some college seminars, the professor has a rule that a student whose phone rings gets a penalty. For example, the student must buy cookies for everybody in the class or the student is marked "absent" for that lecture.

True story: An accounting professor tells his students that the only good reason for them to have their cell phone on 'Ring' is that it's their birthday. So if a student's phone rings, he/she has to say his/her name, and everybody sings "Happy Birthday" to him/her. The result is that very few phones ring during that class.

1. d [0 points]: **Talking on a phone in a restroom:** some people make calls in the office restroom. Perhaps they think it is private there. But cell phones can transmit background noises like flowing water. So even if the restroom has only one toilet, don't occupy it while you make phone calls!

1. e [2 points]: **Talking on a phone in a bus or train** is OK – but only if you talk quietly. When people have to be close together, it's very annoying to listen to someone else's private conversation, whether it is personal or business. In fact, you should be careful what business information you talk about when so many other people can hear: don't talk about confidential matters.

2. a [0 points]: Most Americans **answer their home and cell phones simply by saying** *"Hello."* However, this is not good business etiquette because the caller often doesn't know exactly who is speaking. For the office, see answer **2. e**, next page.

31

ANSWERING THE PHONE

2. b [0 points]: Usually only **the receptionist**, who has the responsibility of answering all general phone calls, should say the name of the company. She usually then asks: *"How may I direct your call?"* or *"May I help you?"* Most companies, however, no longer have a general receptionist but use a voicemail menu instead.

2. c [0 points]: **Don't answer the phone with a last/family name only.** This isn't the custom in North America, and callers won't understand. See answer **2. e**.

2. d [0 points]: No, **don't say *"I am..."*** to answer the phone. Always use the expression *"This is ..."* on the phone. (In person, say *"My name is"* or *"I'm ...".*)

2. e [2 points]: The bookkeeper should **say her full name and department**. This is the best practice for most office workers.

Other options:
- In a very small company without formal departments, Elena would just say her name.
- For informal office cultures, a first name ('Elena') without the last name ('Clinton') might be enough – but not the last name alone.
- If Elena doesn't receive calls from outside the company, then she might not need to say her department name.
- In big companies with lots of calls from unknown customers, on the other hand, office and technical workers sometimes answer with just the name of their department.

POLITENESS ON THE PHONE

3. a [0 points]: **"No" alone is rude** because it is so short, without any polite words. (To say "Yes" is also not helpful in this case because it isn't true, so the customer will be disappointed later when he/she doesn't get the special service.)

3. b [0 points]: Saying **"I don't know" isn't helpful** and is bad for the company's reputation – as if you don't know your job. And avoid the word "problem" with customers because it sounds negative and unsolvable. Use "matter" or "issue" instead.

3. c [**2 points**]: The expression **"I'm afraid that…"** is a polite way to introduce bad news.

3. d [½ **point**]: Most managers will not be happy with your work if you bring them every little problem. The manager hired you to make his/her life easier, not busier! First try to solve this issue by yourself, within the level of responsibility you have. If you cannot, then it might be necessary to go up a level.

Tip: Smiling when you speak: will give your voice a friendly tone. If you are in a customer service job, this can be important, so smile when you talk. However, managers often need to speak more seriously.

PHONING HOME, PHONING YOUR BOSS: CONSIDER THIS

> ### Etiquette and Job Tip: Personal phone calls at work
>
> If you have a phone at or near your desk, you might want to call a family member or make other personal calls sometimes. Most employers allow you to use the company phone for occasional personal calls. However, use a quiet voice to talk with your family, even if you use your cell phone. Loud voices are a major annoyance in cubicle areas; it's not professional behavior. And you shouldn't want your coworkers to know your personal and family problems.
>
> Don't make personal calls often. Making too many personal calls during work time is one of the main office etiquette mistakes that bosses don't like.[7] In some cases it has been a reason to fire an employee. Other examples of bad behavior that can be reason for firing: using swears (offensive language), drinking at work and leaving without permission.

4. a [2 points]: Email is the preferred communication method of senior executives, according to a survey. Two out of three executives prefer email over meetings, memos and phone calls. Emails can be answered when the boss has time. Messages can be stored and the history of an issue can be looked at again later.

4. b, c, d [0 points]: The responses are in order of preference.
- **4. b:** 31% of executives prefer face-to-face meetings.
- **4. c:** 3% of executives like a memo on paper best.
- **4. d:** Only 1% prefer phone messages![8]

In contrast, 2 out of 3 employees who are *not* executives prefer face-to-face contact.[9]

CALL OR TEXT?

4. So if you must leave **a phone message for your boss, speak as clearly and briefly as possible** so that the call isn't too annoying.

5. 1 point for any response(s) listed in <u>a</u> and 1 point for any response(s) listed in <u>b</u>. Total = 2 points

5. a Texting is better:
- when you are answering a text and want to have a record of the message chain.
- when the message is very short and doesn't require a reply, such as *"There in ten"* ("I'll be there in ten minutes.").
- when the recipient can't talk on the phone, for example because he/she is in a meeting.
- when the recipient is in a very noisy environment, such as a construction site.

5. b A phone call can be more appropriate than a text message in some cases, such as:
- in an urgent situation, when you need confirmation that action will be taken.
- for complicated situations, especially when you don't have all the information you need.
- for personal service to a client, making a good impression.
- when the message is sensitive or personal, for example, an apology. Short written texts don't show emotion well.
- when the receiver regularly doesn't respond to texts.

Regarding age and smartphone use: A survey in 2013 showed that people over age sixty use their phones 40 percent of the time for talking and only 25 percent for texting. But people under thirty use them to over 50 percent for texting and only 12 percent for phone calls.[10]

35

PHONE ETIQUETTE

6. a [2 points] "a doctor's appointment": This is <u>not</u> appropriate because the reason for not answering the phone is too personal. Your health is a private, not a company, matter.

6. b-d [0 points]: These three messages represent <u>good voicemail etiquette</u>. They tell the caller:
- why you can't respond to their call, with a business-appropriate reason
- when you will return
- when they can expect a reply or who will call back

6. e: 0 points because option **a** is not appropriate.

7. a, b, c, e [0 points]: **When you are trying to reach someone,** it is OK to follow up the first phone message. But don't call too often (more than once a day) because it is seen as being impatient and aggressive. And if you wait too long (two to three days), you might not remember the details of the call.

7. d [2 points]: One day later you can make a second (follow-up) phone call if you don't connect with someone on the first call. It might be better to follow up the phone call with an email.

> **Tip: Good etiquette also means patience and good listening skills**: Don't be quick to think someone is being rude to you. In multicultural workplaces and multinational companies, customs of your phone partner might be different from your own. Good listening skills are important for successful phone calls.

MULTITASKING

8. a, b [1/2 point]: Some people think that multitasking is completely inefficient, while others believe that they can do it well. See the **8. c** for the research findings.

8. c [2 points]: Multitasking can only be done successfully when the tasks don't require a lot of thinking, not for complicated tasks.[11] For example, it isn't effective to write an email message while you are also talking about something else on the phone.

Many people multitask often during the day and night, especially young people. Almost every second employee checks his/her smartphone at work at least once every hour.[12] Recent research also shows that when people check Facebook or other social networking sites while they are working, they are thinking of two different things at the same time. If they try to get more tasks done by constantly flipping through different screens on the computer, they will actually be less productive.[13]

More research shows that people remember less information when they are multitasking. It is hard to learn effectively then, too.[14] A recent study found that constant information overload – email, instant messaging, phone calls – can lower a worker's IQ by ten points on average.[15]

Job Tip: Take a break

Today it is common for professionals and knowledge workers to tackle one task after another all day long. If that happens quickly and often enough, it affects their productivity negatively.

You need time to stop thinking about one task before going on to another[16] – so taking a break can be a habit that helps you to be more productive.

HOW TO SAY IT: OFFICE VOICEMAIL GREETINGS

SIX POINTS OF VOICEMAIL ETIQUETTE

The six points below represent good voicemail etiquette, especially for people who have to co-ordinate others or respond to clients and urgent situations.

Start by saying your name slowly, then tell the caller:

1. what day the message was recorded, so they know it's current

2. that you can't respond to their call right now – and perhaps say why not, if it's appropriate and not too personal

3. when you'll return

4. whether you will pick up your messages today

5. when they can expect a reply

6. what they can do if they have an urgent message

SAMPLE OFFICE VOICEMAIL GREETING

"You have reached the voicemail of Sunny Chan, *Client Services.*"
    Formula: "You have reached the voicemail of" + Firstname Lastname, X Department.

"*I am not at my desk today, April 11th, until four p.m.*"
    Formula: **place** - **date** - **time** [a.m./p.m.]

"*Please leave me a message after the tone.*"
    [Or: *after the beep*]

"*I'll get back to you as soon as possible this afternoon or tomorrow.*"
    Formula: "I'll get back to you" + time or date

Where needed: "*If this message is urgent, please press zero. The receptionist will redirect your call.*"

ACTION:
1. Call some companies after hours and listen to their voicemail greetings to get ideas about typical content. Besides vocabulary, listen to the intonation (sentence melody).

2. Record a voicemail greeting for your work or imaginary job. Use the points and sample script above, or greetings you listened to, as models.

UNIT 3
MAKING A GOOD FIRST IMPRESSION
WITH EMAIL

Business people often connect with each other by email before they meet in person. The first email you send can make either a good or bad impression.

In this unit you will find answers to questions like:

- Is sending an email the best way to communicate at work?

- How do you begin a business email – *Dear..., Hello, Hi*? And how do you close?

- What are some common abbreviations used in business emails?

- Is it OK to check personal email at work?

 Key words: *recipient, Subject line, abbreviation, address a person, Ms., closing, monitor, browse/browsing*

There are 8 questions and 16 points in this unit.

1. Business communication: email or phone call?

In what business situations is it better to write an email than make a phone call?

Email is better when: _____

_____

_____

_____

_____

2. Most people answer their personal emails and texts right away. How about work emails?

How soon after receiving an email should an office worker respond to it? Choose the best answer.
[Note: This question is for general office workers, not special groups, like sales representatives or company presidents.]

☐ **a.** immediately, within an hour

☐ **b.** in 2-4 hours

☐ **c.** in the same workday or within 24 hours

☐ **d.** within the work week

3. Office workers receive (too) many emails. To help the recipient decide what is urgent, and to get a reply when you need one, it is good etiquette to note in the Subject line whether action is needed or not.

The following email Subject lines refer to a client (AB) file.

QUESTION: Which one of the messages requires a response from the reader?

☐ **a.** AB file closed today – e.o.m.

☐ **b.** Dinner meeting with AB Thurs. 6:30 – RSVP

☐ **c.** FYI: AB file update

☐ **d.** P.S. to AB file – NRN

Note: If you aren't sure of the abbreviations above, see the "HOW TO WRITE IT" section at the end of this chapter.

4. When is the greeting *"Dear...[Name]"* an appropriate way to start a business email?

☐ **a.** When writing to a new client or someone higher up in the company – it shows respect.

☐ **b.** When writing to almost anyone – it's a common email greeting.

☐ **c.** Don't use "Dear" as an email greeting – it's only appropriate for business letters (on paper).

5. How do you address a person of respect whom you don't know well in an email? For example, to make a good impression in an email to a professor whose name is Gita Dallakoti, which greeting(s) can you use? Check <u>all</u> appropriate options:

☐ **a.** *Dear Professor Dallakoti,*

☐ **b.** *Dear Ms. Dallakoti,*

☐ **c.** *Dear Gita Dallakoti,*

☐ **d.** *Dear Dallakoti,*

☐ **e.** *To Mrs. Gita,*

☐ **f.** *Hello Gita,*

6. When closing (ending) a business email, which word or expression is common for which situation? For each email situation on the left (a, b, c), choose a closing expression on the right; more than one response might be OK but choose the best one. Write its number in the corresponding box.

In an email to:	use this:
☐ a. an important client about a serious topic	1. *Yours truly,*
☐ b. a close coworker	2. *Regards,*
☐ c. anyone – almost always appropriate	3. *With great respect I remain Yours truly,*
	4. *No closing expression. The email ends with the final sentence and writer's name.*

7. Is it OK to use a company computer* to check personal email or the news online or do some quick internet banking during work time?

☐ **a. Yes. I should have the flexibility** to spend a little personal time on the company computer during working hours whenever I need to.

☐ **b. Yes. When I have no important work to do**, it's OK to browse/surf the Web for a short time, for example, to check personal email. But only when work is slow, and only for important reasons.

☐ **c.** It's OK to do online banking, etc., on the company computer **during my lunch break**, but never during actual work time.

☐ **d. No.** My computer and access to the internet are provided by my employer for work reasons only; so **I don't use them for personal reasons.** I use my own devices if I want to go online during my lunch hour.

Note: The best answers to Questions 7 and 8 might be different if the company doesn't provide a computer but instead has a policy of BYOD (bring your own device, e.g., laptop or smartphone).

8. Does your employer have the right to monitor/check your **work email** and the **browsing history** on your work computer?

☐ **a. No**. Employers don't have those rights in Canada and the United States.

☐ **b. Yes, but...:** Employers have the right to check both but few companies actually do it.

☐ **c. Yes**. Employers have the right to check both – and more than half of them use that right.

Cultural Note: Why do some people send so many emails?

It's easy, and lazy, to just hit "Reply to all" when you answer an email. And it feels as if a lot of work has been accomplished. Those are certainly some reasons why many people do it. However, there could be a cultural reason in our multicultural offices as well.

In most countries, society is quite collective, meaning that groups are very important. People identify themselves as members of a group, for example, an extended family or the company that they work for. Employees who have work experience in collective cultures are used to sending a lot of email. They send messages to everybody who could possibly be affected by, or interested in, the content.[17] In the same way, they like to receive replies to their email. They might feel left out or snubbed if they are not copied often.

In contrast, North American culture is rather individualistic, meaning that the individuals and their rights and interests are more important than the group. Children are taught early to make choices by themselves. Adults, and employees at all levels, are expected to be relatively independent and responsible and not to rely on a group very much. The North American view is that emails should be directed only to people who need to act on them. They prefer not to use the "Reply to all" button.

UNIT 3. ANSWERS:

Point scores are a little different in this unit:

2 points for 2b, 3b, 4a, 7c.

1 point for these answers: any response listed in #1 (below), 2c, 5a, 5b, 6a "1", 6b "4", 6c "2" (see page 56), 7b, 7d.

½ point for #1 any response that isn't listed below, and 6a "2", 6b "2".

WRITE YOUR SCORE HERE. → → → ☐

1. 1 point if you wrote any response(s) listed here; ½ point for another response; 0 points if you wrote nothing.
When to email, when to call: **Email is better...**

- for most cases when the receiver (for example, an executive) prefers email.
- when the recipient can't be reached by a phone call, for example, in a meeting or overseas, or you don't have their phone number.
- when you want to reach many people at once.
- when you are answering an email and want to refer to the original message.
- when the message contains detailed information that is difficult to say over the phone.
- when you want to have the written record.
- to send an attachment.

Most business people receive emails as well as calls on their smart phone.

2. a [0 points]: Some people feel stressed if they don't answer their email immediately. Too much stress at work can lead to health problems. **Relax: in most jobs it isn't usually necessary to answer immediately.**

EMAIL WRITING

2. a continued: Sales representatives, real estate agents, etc. are often an exception. They often need to be quick to respond to clients and customers, so they carry smart phones with them all the time. Some other professionals, such as accountants, might also work in a company culture that demands very quick responses.

2. b [2 points]: It is good email etiquette to try to **answer your daytime email within four hours, or a half-day.** If you are away from your email for several hours or a day or more, then update your "Out-of-office" message. This informs your partners that your response will be delayed. **Email that is sent to you after work hours:** company expectations about after-hours emails vary. Be sure you know what your boss expects. A good boss will explain and also listen to your point of view.

2. c [1 point]: In some jobs, responding to an email in 24 hours is fine.

2. d [0 points]: The North American business culture is fast-paced and time-sensitive. Waiting several days or a week to respond doesn't make a good impression.

3. a [0 points]: e.o.m. means "end of message." This abbreviation isn't as common as the others in this list. It is used a lot within some companies and not at all in others.

3. b [2 points]: RSVP means "please respond to this invitation." It always requires a reply – Yes or No that you will attend. (Originally French for "répondez s'il vous plaît," the abbreviation is widely used in English.)

EMAIL STRESS

3. c, d [0 points]: These emails don't require action, and it's good etiquette to make that clear in the Subject line:

- **FYI** means "for your information," so recipients can just read it and don't need to take action.

- **NRN** means "no return/response necessary."

Email distractions

In the office, most employees have a lot of distractions around them. **Incoming email is one of the biggest distractions.** The average North American business person gets almost 100 emails per day – around the world more than one hundred twenty million business emails are sent daily.[18] Reading and writing them takes more than two hours of work time every work day.

Office employees sitting at their computer typically check incoming email thirty to forty times per hour,[19] often interrupting another activity. But every time they stop other work to check an incoming email, it can take about 15 minutes afterwards to return to full concentration on the original task.[20] To reduce interruptions due to in-house messages, some companies have bulletin boards where all messages to "Everybody" or "Staff" are posted, rather than going directly into individual mailboxes.

Emailing can take so much time that some big companies (Intel, for example) have tried naming one day a week a **"no-email day."**[21] No-email days can be successful and productive if the top managers support them. Sometimes, however, it takes a while for workers to get used to it.

EMAIL GREETINGS: "DEAR"

4. a [2 points]: *"Dear"* **can be used with new contacts** in those cases when the email is written in the style of a formal letter. Within a company it might be used to a senior manager whom you have never met, or when you make a formal request, but it is rather rare nowadays in in-house emails. Many managers want to have good, even friendly, relations with their staff and don't mind casual greetings in emails and in the office. Less formal greetings that are common include *Hello* and *Hi*.

4. b [0 points] No. *"Dear"* isn't very common nowadays.

4. c [0 points] While *"Dear"* is used in letters, it can also be appropriate for rather formal emails – see above.

5. For notes on Punctuation in greetings, see HOW TO WRITE IT, page 59.

5. a, b [1 point each]: These are correct ways to address someone formally and semi-formally in writing. A title, such as *Professor, Dr., Ms., Mr.,* is followed by a last name. However, nowadays *Dr.* and *Professor* are not always used, as the academic environment isn't very formal, so *Ms.* or *Mr.* might be used instead.

Ms. **for a woman** is the same as *Mr.* for a man – it doesn't show whether the person is married or not. *Ms.* is the most acceptable greeting title for women in business correspondence.

MORE EMAIL GREETINGS

Note that other **professions**, such as engineer or lawyer, are not titles in North America; so *Dear Engineer Dallakoti* would not be appropriate. (There are some exceptions to these rules for diplomats, leading politicians, and royalty.)

5. c [0 points]: *"Dear Gita Dallakoti,"* is an impersonal greeting. This kind of greeting is mostly used for mass mailings, where the sender doesn't know the recipient or doesn't care whether the recipient is male or female. It isn't recommended for emails where you want to make a personal connection. And don't use it when you know the recipient personally; it shows a lack of sincere interest.

5. d [0 points]: A last name cannot be used without a title.

5. e [0 points]: A first name cannot be used with a title (*Mrs.*). As well, *"To"* is not a common way to start an email except for the impersonal *"To whom it concerns:"* which is used when you don't know the name of the recipient, for example, in applying for a job.

5. f [0 points]: *"Hello Gita,"* is less formal. If you don't know the recipient well, then avoid this casual greeting for the first email to a person of higher rank. For later emails, follow the recipient's style: If he/she signs with full name and title, then continue to use greetings such as in **5. a** and **b** above. Often a recipient will sign a response with a first name only; in that case you can use this greeting *(Hello + First name)* in your reply.

EMAIL CLOSINGS

6. There are three points in total for this question.

6. a [1 point for "1"; ½ point for "2"]: Messages to clients and customers should always end with a closing expression and an e-signature or typed name. As a closing, *Yours truly* (1) is quite formal and therefore often used with clients in serious cases and for legal matters. On the other hand, *Regards* (2) is an option but it's rather short for a new client and a serious email.

6. b [1 point for "4"; ½ point for "2"]: No closing expression (4): The sender simply writes his/her name after the final sentence (but sometimes omits it). This is quite common in inner-office emails and memos, since sender and recipient know each other well. *Regards* (2), again, is possible; but staff who work closely together often don't need the formality of any closing.

6. c [1 point for "2"]: *Regards* (2) (or *Best regards*) is the most common business email closing. It can be used for everybody at work, although sometimes other closings may be more appropriate, as in **a** and **b** above. (Note: The common closing for a business letter, *Sincerely,* is a little more formal and not used so much in emails.)

Cultural Note: Email closings

The third expression, *With great respect, I remain, Yours faithfully*, is not appropriate in North America. This kind of long expression is not used at all – neither in letters nor in emails. The same is true for *Yours in service*. These expressions may be appropriate in other cultures, but in North America they sound out of place, and they don't make a good impression on the reader.

EMPLOYERS' RIGHTS

7. These answers reflect current trends for use of a company computer at work. For BYOD ("bring your own device") workplaces, security, and legal policies are still developing.

7. a [½ point]: Some employers allow browsing because they don't want to be too strict. They want to show that they trust their staff. However, **most companies aren't so flexible**; they have some restrictions on personal use of a company computer at work. Because, around the globe, some employees browse too much – e.g. one to two hours per day, following news and social media or shopping – some companies block these sites. [22]

> **True story**: *The City of Toronto found internet abuse among its employees. In 2006 two hundred employees (2% of city workers) spent more than two hours per day surfing for personal reasons. The City had to make new, strict rules.*

7. b [½ point]: **Check with your employer** whether it's OK to surf the internet and answer personal emails when work is slow, even if you see some coworkers doing it.

7. c [2 points]: **Lunchtime is your own time**, and for many companies, it is OK to use the office computer for personal reasons then. Noon to 2:00 is the time that online TV [23] and puzzles [24] are most often accessed.

7. d [1 point]: In some companies, **employees can't use their work computer for personal reasons**. RBC Bank is an example. In 2007 they explained that "Internet access and email are provided to employees as a tool for their business needs," with few exceptions allowed. [25]

COMPANY EMAIL POLICIES

8 a, b [0 points]: Wrong answer.

8. c [2 points]: Companies have the right to use monitoring software on computers that they own. About two thirds of Canadian companies actively monitor their employees' computer use. They can monitor what internet sites you have visited and block sites. They can also check how many minutes you spend on each site. They can check what you say about your job on social media sites as well.

Employers monitor their workers' browsing not just because of lost work hours. While online banking is relatively harmless, illegal site visits are not. Sites that can be illegal at work include pornography. An employee who abuses company internet rules can be fired.

What do employees think about this? Half of them think that companies should not have that right.[26] On the other hand, 29 percent say their coworkers surf the internet too much, so employers *should* monitor![27]

Every company should have a clear policy on personal internet surfing at work. It should include:

- what is allowed (e.g, personal use during lunch time?)
- what is not allowed (specific internet sites and email content)
- how internet use will be monitored by the company, for example, what software the company uses to check and record internet history
- what the consequences will be if you don't follow company rules.

HOW TO WRITE IT: PUNCTUATION AND ABBREVIATIONS FOR EMAILS

PUNCTUATION

Business email openings can be followed by a comma or a colon. A colon is a little more formal than a comma.
- Dear Mr. Jones:
- Hi Tina,

An exclamation point (!) after a greeting is casual:
- Hi Suzie!
and best for friends only, not business associates.

Most closings are followed by a comma:
- Regards,
(Note that this North American custom differs from the British style of no comma.) Your name is on a separate line below the closing expression. Contact information is below your name.

Some informal closing expressions may be followed by one, but only one, exclamation point, like:
- *Cheers!*
Unlike telephone calls and face-to-face meetings, written messages don't deliver much emotion. An exclamation point can help to show joy or surprise. However, it isn't good business email etiquette to use more than one exclamation point anywhere. Using two or more -- !! -- represents too much emotion, like jumping up and down and shouting.

Another way to show feelings with punctuation is with **smiley faces** ☺, ☹, using a colon with a right or left parenthesis, :) These face pictures are also called *emojis* or *emoticons*. They are fine in emails and text messages to friends and social contacts, where they add personal feeling. But most people find that smileys, like multiple exclamation points, look unprofessional in business correspondence. Try using words instead: *"I'm happy to say that..."/"I'm sorry to hear that..."* -- or a phone call.

A message written in **ALL CAPITAL LETTERS** looks emotional, too. It looks as if the writer is shouting at the recipient, which produces a negative reaction in the reader. Use capitals only where they are needed: for names, the word *"I"* and at the beginning of sentences.

ABBREVIATIONS

Abbreviations are short forms of words, often just one letter instead of the whole word. Many of them have been used in writings for centuries and come from the Latin language. While each occupation or industry has its own specific abbreviations, some common ones punctuated with periods are:

e.g. *for example* [introduces an example] [from Latin] Do not confuse with *i.e.* below.

e.o.m. *end of message* [at the end of the Subject line when there is no text below] Also: *eom.*

etc. *and more of the same, and similar things* [from Latin]

F.Y.I. *For your information.* [often used for an email with background information that does not need a reply] Also without periods: FYI

i.e.   *that is* [introduces a restatement of the previous thought, using different words] [from Latin] Do not confuse with *e.g.*; *i.e.* is not for examples.

P.S.   *post script* [introduces something added after the signature] [from Latin]

R.S.V.P.   *please reply* [at the end of an invitation] [French] A response is required. Also: *RSVP*

Some abbreviations and short forms don't need periods – it's just not the custom:

ASAP, asap   *as soon as possible, very soon/quickly*

NRN   *No return necessary. Don't reply to this message.*

pls   *please*

re   *about, regarding, in reference to*

rec'd   *received*

thx   *thanks*

Short forms in informal emails:

Some informal emails look like text messages. Text messaging has brought many new short forms. They increase and change very quickly, so it's impossible to list here all the informal abbreviations that are used today. Here is a sample; the long text appears at the bottom of the next page:

• hi, m not cmg 2 mtg. c u l8r.

> **Tip: Good writing skills** are important in business. Research[28] shows that:
>
> - when new employees at big accountant firms lose their jobs, it is mainly because they can't write well.
> - university students who are good writers later earn more than three times the salary (on average) of weak student writers.

◆

Now go to page 191 and enter your scores for Part 1 in the chart. Add them up and see how good your business soft skills were when you started this book. Now, of course, after reading all the solutions, you know more about making a good impression in person, on the phone and by email!

◆

ACTION:

Write an email to an instructor, employment resource centre, city administration or LinkedIn group member (not FaceBook because communications there are casual). Your email should make a good impression and ask a question that requires a response. The reply will provide a real example of business email style.

Solution to text message on the previous page:

Hi. I am not coming to the meeting. See you later.

Part 2

SOFT SKILLS FOR GETTING ALONG IN THE OFFICE

UNIT 4
SMALL TALK AND SOCIALIZING

In this unit you will find answers to questions like:

- Is it OK to compliment coworkers on their nice clothes?

- Is it OK to date a coworker?

- What should you talk about at a business dinner?

 Key words: *small talk, compliment, inappropriate, dating, manners, business dinner, dress code, bilingual, diversity*

There are 8 questions and 16 points in this unit.

1. SITUATION: Common greetings in the office are:

- How're things?
- How's it going?
- What's up?

You can answer in lots of ways – for example, three of the answers below are fine.

QUESTION: Which one of the answers is _not_ the best business etiquette?

☐ **a.** *"Fine."*

☐ **b.** *"Everything's good, thanks."*

☐ **c.** *"OK, except my car broke down, and I'm taking the bus this week."*

☐ **d.** *"Busy! No time to talk right now, but I'll catch you later."*

2. How do you address a <u>new</u> coworker or colleague at work, by first name or family name?

☐ **a.** It depends on gender: Men can use first names with other men but not with women, and women can use first names with other women but not with men.

☐ **b.** You should almost always say "Mr./Ms. Lastname" to a new colleague. Proper etiquette means you have to wait for the colleague to suggest that you use first names.

☐ **c.** You can almost always use the first name. North Americans are casual about names.

3. SITUATION: Everybody likes to make a good impression. And it's nice to show that you notice individuals by complimenting them then.

QUESTION: Which one of the following should you probably not compliment?

☐ **a.** your coworker's new blouse

☐ **b.** your coworker's new bag, briefcase or purse

☐ **c.** your coworker's presentation on a new project

☐ **d.** the food your coworker brought to the company party

4. SITUATION: Isabella is going to make a presentation to a client company in the afternoon, so she wears a short dress that she doesn't usually wear at work. The team leader compliments her, saying: "Wow, you look great! We'll certainly get the contract now!"

☐ **a.** The team leader is making a nice compliment.

☐ **b.** The team leader's compliment is not appropriate.

☐ **c.** The appropriateness of the comment depends on whether the team leader is a man or a woman.

5. Can office socializing include dating coworkers?

SITUATION: Dana was hired by ABC Company six months ago. Chris has been working there for three years and is a supervisor. Dana and Chris have recently been spending their lunchtime together. They are also both members of a team, where they work well together. In fact, they are becoming romantically interested in each other and want to date. (They are both single.)

QUESTION: Is it OK for these office colleagues to date each other?

☐ **a. No**. Romance has no place at work, especially between team members. If they want to date or be lovers, then Dana, who was more recently hired, should find another job.

☐ **b. They should be very careful** about dating. Chris is a supervisor and might become Dana's boss some day. If they are in love, Chris would not be able to direct Dana objectively.

☐ **c. Sure, no problem**. People spend a lot of time at work, so it's not surprising that they sometimes fall in love. Many people meet their future spouses at the office. Everybody loves a romance.

Note: Dana and Chris are names for both men and women, so consider all the possible dating situations.

6. SITUATION: You're new at this company. Several of your new coworkers tell you that they have a good boss, Lasantha.

QUESTION: Which of the coworkers do you think you can trust for good information and advice?
(More than one answer might be good, but choose just one.)

☐ **a.** Aaron: "Lasantha is the most beautiful boss I've ever worked for!"

☐ **b.** Bobby: "Lasantha is a great boss. If you're not feeling great some day, like maybe you have a hangover, she doesn't bother you. You can just take it easy that day."

☐ **c.** Cameron: "Lasantha is a great boss. If you have a question or suggestion, she'll find time to listen to you."

☐ **d.** Dale: "Lasantha's a good boss. Poor woman – she's got allergies, though. So we can't have any flowers in the office. Of course, that's fine with me, because I have terrible allergies myself. I think we might even have a sick building here. Somebody's always coughing or sneezing. You know, I advise you to keep tissues at your desk."

☐ **e.** E.J.: "Lasantha is all right. You know, she's not originally from here, though, and some of us think John should have been promoted instead of her."

7. SITUATION: X is an employee who immigrated to Toronto, Canada several years ago. She shares the office with three others; one speaks her language and two speak only English. X speaks English quite well but she often feels like using her first language in the office to talk with the coworker from her country.

QUESTION: Do you think she should speak her first language in the four-person office?
(You might agree with more than one answer but choose just one.)

☐ **a. Yes,** there is no reason *not* to speak her first language. Coworkers who don't speak X's language should not complain. It's good for X and her colleague to continue to practice their language.

☐ **b. No, it's never polite** to speak a language that isn't English in the shared office. It's very annoying. People who speak only English should complain to X and her colleagues and ask them to stop it. X has a responsibility to speak English.

☐ **c. It's not very good manners.** Coworkers who don't speak X's language might feel bad if they can't understand what X and her group are talking about. They should explain their feelings to X; and she should be kind and speak English.

☐ **d.** English-speaking colleagues should patiently **support X when she speaks English.** They have a co-responsibility to make sure that everyone is included in discussions.

8. SITUATION: You are at a business dinner with clients or potential clients of the company.

QUESTION: Should there be conversation during this business meal?

☐ **a. Not much.** Conversation is better after the meal is finished.

☐ **b.** Yes, there should be **small talk**, for example, about the weather, sports or festivals. No business or personal topics.

☐ **c.** Yes, there should be conversation that **includes personal information about families** so that strong relationships can be made. No business topics.

☐ **d.** Yes, the host will direct the conversation. It will often start with **small talk and family topics.** It will usually **also include business topics,** which are the reason for the meal together.

UNIT 4. SMALL TALK AND SOCIALIZING

ANSWERS:
2 points for: 1a, 2c, 3a, 4b, 5b, 6c, 7c, 7d, 8d
1 point for these answers: 5a, 7a; and ½ point for 5c

☐   ←   ←   ← WRITE YOUR SCORE HERE

1. a [2 points]: The answer that is NOT good etiquette is a **one-word answer** to a greeting. One-word responses can sound rude because they make small talk impossible. In fact, people might think you don't like them if you answer with only a word or two.

Note: These questions are different from *"How are you?"* These are informal questions about your life in general, not your health. After *"How are you?"* a real conversation isn't expected; a one- or two-word answer (*"Fine. You?"*) is OK.

Cultural Note: Greetings and small talk

Greetings can be very brief for English-speaking North Americans. But in some cultures in our multicultural workforce, there is always a follow-up question: *"How's the family?"* The asker may be used to having a five-to-ten minute conversation in his/her country of origin; but a North American office worker will most likely give only a short answer.

---

1. b, c, d [0 points – the question asked which answer is NOT good]: **Answers b, c, d are all good responses** to *"What's up?"* and similar greetings. Use your soft skills to connect with coworkers and others through small talk like this. These questions are open-ended, so that you can give a longer answer which invites a conversation.

SMALL TALK IN THE OFFICE

Positive responses to greetings can help you get along, build networks, and maintain good customer relationships, in person or on the phone. Your answer to a greeting should be **positive** if possible, like **1. b** (*"Everything's good, thanks"*). But you can also mention some news that is not so positive, like **1. c** (*"OK, except my car broke down"*), as long as it is not a very personal, sensitive subject. A response about being busy, like **1. d**, isn't rude if it concludes with a positive remark like *"catch you later."*

Small talk should be friendly. Negative remarks, for example about:
- big, sensitive, personal problems (debt, divorce, etc.)
- criticisms of coworkers or bosses
- complaints about your company don't belong in office conversations. Coworkers often avoid people who give everybody a bad mood by being negative all the time.

True story: *A new immigrant from Germany complained: "Since I've been in Canada, my lips are so tired at the end of the day! It seems like I have to stretch them into a smile at the office all day. It feels so unnatural." After a few weeks, however, he got used to this way of showing friendliness.*

FIRST NAMES WITH NEW EMPLOYEES

> **Job Tip: If you are shy** about talking with coworkers, try to be the first one to speak. Ask a question like "How're things?" when you see someone you would like to talk to. Then that person has to answer, and you have time to listen and plan your own response. By listening, you can get to know your colleagues better. You might find that you share some interests, which you can talk more about in the future.

2. a, b [0 points]: **Coworkers are equals** and introductions are gender-neutral, as seen in Unit 1. It's not necessary to always wait for an invitation to use a coworker's first name. You can assume first names are OK.

2. c [2 points]: **Most business people use first names** right away (*"Nice to meet you, Neil."*) in North America – except sometimes when junior employees are meeting senior managers. This contrasts with customs in countries where junior staff always address higher-ranked staff with "Sir" or "Madam." (In some parts of the world, "Sir" is used for higher-ranking men *and women* – that would be very confusing in North America, where "Sir" is always male.)

> **Cultural Note: Men may use last names**
>
> Sometimes men call each other by their last names without "Mr." For example, *"How's everything, Smith?"* Since athletes often do this, men who follow this custom might be thinking of their colleagues as team mates. The custom isn't so common among women.

COMPLIMENTS

3. a [2 points]: At work it is usually *not* appropriate to compliment a colleague, especially a woman, on attractiveness or clothing on the body – unless you are friends. See the Etiquette tip box below.

3. b, c, d [0 points]: It is OK to make a compliment about good work, helpful contributions to a party or items like bags or jewelry. In fact, most employees would be very glad to receive a compliment about work they did well.

The correct response to a compliment is: *Thank you* or *Thanks.*

Etiquette Tip: Compliments at work

It is nice to compliment any staff member on their **work** when they do a good job. That is a professional comment.

Usually it's <u>not</u> OK to compliment someone on appearance, how he/she looks or dresses. That is a personal comment, which is not proper work etiquette – unless you are **friends as well as coworkers.**

Making personal comments on colleagues' or assistants' attractiveness can be considered sexual harassment – whether the speaker is a man or a woman.

---

4. a and **c** [0 points]: Whether the team leader is a man or a woman, the comment to Isabella is not appropriate -- see the Etiquette tip box above.

TOO PERSONAL

4. b [2 points]: Isabella's team leader made a personal comment about her appearance, not a professional compliment. If the team leader is a man, it makes the comment worse, because it can be considered sexual harassment. But it is also wrong for a woman to say this. Isabella can complain to a manager, especially if she feels uncomfortable or if her team leader makes similar comments often.

If she wants to respond to the team leader with good soft skills, Isabella can say something like, "*You mean that my presentation will impress them, I hope/ I'm sure.*" She can also say that the comment is offensive to her (if it is).

Isabella should also ask herself whether she chose an appropriate dress. Are the clients going to notice her body more than her ideas? If so, then she is not dressed professionally. She should check her company's dress code [rules of what is appropriate to wear]. See page 17 for more information about appropriate business clothing.

5. Can office socializing include dating coworkers? People have different opinions on this question.

5. a [1 point]: Some people say that **romance has no place at work**. This rule may be best for the company, especially if the number of employees is small, and they all work closely together.

In Canada, 22 percent of employees report that their company has a policy against office romances.[29] However, for the couple it isn't easy to decide that one person has to leave the job and find another one.

OFFICE ROMANCE: YES OR NO?

5. b [2 points]: Managers are concerned when there is a love affair in the office. People in love cannot be objective, they say. Other employees can complain if there is any favoritism. That is especially important when one person has a position that supervises or manages the other person. (See also answer **c**.) In fact, about one in four U.S. companies ask employees to register an office romance. The couple then must promise not to behave unprofessionally in the office or on company business.[30]

5. c [½ point]: Although almost all young workers think it's no problem, **actually there can be many problems** with an office romance or affair. While it's true that some people meet their future spouse at work, answer **c** does not recognize the dangers of an office romance. For example, coworkers could feel jealous of the lovers; or they could just be distracted from their work. Often romances don't lead to permanent happiness. See answer **b**, too. For all these reasons, an office affair or romance could easily result in a bad working environment.

Friends matter

Educational background has an influence on a person's salary. Now research shows that financial success depends not on education alone but also on number of friends: For every year of education past high school, people's salaries increase five percent. And for "every extra friend a pupil had at school, their salary 35 years later was two percent higher."[31]

OFFICE SOFT SKILLS: WORKING WITH NORTH AMERICANS

PRAISE FOR THE BOSS SAYS SOMETHING ABOUT THE SPEAKER

6. a [0 points]: Aaron's comment *("Lasantha is the most beautiful boss I've ever worked for!")* isn't professional – beauty is not a professional qualification. Aaron might be sexist; that means he makes inappropriate distinctions between men and women on the job. Or he might just be an 'airhead', a person who doesn't think much before speaking. In either case, Aaron can't be trusted for the best advice.

6. b [0 points]: You can guess that Bobby has had unproductive days when he had a hangover. He might have a drinking problem or might just be lazy, a 'slacker'. Until you find out more about him, it isn't a very good idea to be good friends with someone who doesn't always do his work well.

6. c [2 points]: Cameron's reason why Lasantha is a good boss *("If you have a question or suggestion, she'll find time to listen to you.")* is professional, not personal. Cameron will probably give professional advice in the future, too.

6. d [0 points]: Dale is a complainer and maybe a gossiper. He or she likes to complain about health problems (allergies and *"Somebody's always coughing or sneezing."*). Colleagues with a negative attitude often infect others with that bad attitude. This isn't a good person to seek advice from. His/Her advice will probably be negative.

COMMUNICATING ACROSS CULTURES

6. e [0 points]: E.J. is also a complainer and not happy with this boss. In fact, E.J. seems to be prejudiced against people "not originally from here." This comment is culturally discriminatory. It is completely inappropriate and can be a reason for dismissal from the company. E.J. might also be sexist, since he/she would prefer John to Lasantha. Don't seek advice from someone like E.J.!

7. It is an advantage to be able to speak two or more languages and have multiple world views. Many companies today are happy to hire employees who speak the languages of their customers and clients. But it's not always appropriate to speak other languages at work.

7. a [1 point]: **It's OK for immigrants to speak their first language in the office.** If you chose this answer, you're very tolerant. You recognize that a person's first language is an important part of his/her self-identity.

However, let's think further about what happens when X and her same-language colleagues speak non-English in the office. Their conversation can't be understood by everyone. This is not an issue of political correctness but of manners and politeness: it is not polite to exclude other people around you when you speak. Just like whispering, this could be a problem; it could cause a bad atmosphere in the office.

As well, if X and her group always sit and talk together, eat their own food, and separate themselves from others, they might not easily connect with other colleagues during work time.

BILINGUAL COWORKERS

7. a continued: X has to ask herself whether she wants her colleagues to see her only as a member of her first-language group and not as a member of the whole office group or team. In a business workplace, that can become a problem for management.

So answer **a** has some good points but it isn't the only good response.

7. b [0 points]: **"It's never polite" is too strongly negative.** A company cannot make rules about language use in private time, like break times. Everyone has rights in the workplace, not just the English-speaking coworkers. And even if X's English-speaking coworkers think she is rude, a complaint isn't constructive and does not make friends.

7. c [2 points]: Talk about it. When X speaks a language they can't understand, coworkers will probably wonder what she is talking about. They might be worried that she is gossiping about them or saying things she doesn't want them to hear. It is best if everyone can talk sincerely and explain their feelings politely. If a conversation begins, it can result in better understanding among everyone. X might not even realize how often she speaks her first language. Perhaps she hasn't thought about others' feelings when she speaks her mother tongue.

Some companies also have a language policy or diversity committee to help with these issues and discrimination in general.[32] Coworkers who talk about this together learn to understand different views.

CONVERSATION IN THE OFFICE AND AT BUSINESS DINNERS

7. d [2 points]: While **c** is a good answer, it is also correct that **English-speaking coworkers have a responsibility** to include X in teamwork and friendly conversations. That might mean they need a little patience. In the same way, it's better for everyone if X, too, can show that she is willing and happy to have English-speaking coworkers join her discussions.

8. a, b, and c [0 points]: It may be the custom in some other cultures to **avoid business topics** – or avoid talking at all – during a business dinner. But this is not the North American custom.

8. d [2 points]: It is OK to talk about business issues during a business meal, as well as small talk and some (happy) family matters. The host usually directs the conversation and includes even junior guests. The conversation can begin with general topics and turn to business later. The host usually begins the business talk, but sometimes the guest does this.

HOW TO SAY IT: RESPONDING TO INVITATIONS

There are many occasions in your career when you will receive an invitation. These can be personal, for example, a colleague's birthday party, or work-related, such as an orientation meeting, AGM (Annual General Meeting) or company picnic. Most invitations require a reply.

a) R.S.V.P./RSVP

Written invitations (paper or email) for big events often end with "R.S.V.P." As explained in Unit 3, the expression is from the French for "please respond." It has been used for more than a century, since French became known in Europe as the language of diplomacy. It means that the sender asks you to tell them whether you are coming or not.

When "*R.S.V.P. Regrets*" or "*Regrets only*" is added to an invitation, it means that you only need to respond if you are NOT going to attend. In other words, you *regret* that you cannot attend. The sender expects that everyone who does not reply will come.

If you receive a note or invitation with "RSVP" on it, it is very rude, or thoughtless, not to reply. The sender requires responses from everyone in order to make arrangements for the correct number of guests.

b) Accepting an invitation

Many invitations are sent by email; and you can reply by email. A long response isn't expected. You can just write:
- "*I'll be there.*"
- "*Great! See you there.*"
- "*Looking forward to it.*"

Before you hit 'Reply to Sender,' add a few words like those above to the Subject line of the email to indicate whether you are accepting or declining the invitation. That helps the event organizer to know immediately whether to count you in or out.

Your response can be the same if the invitation is spoken, in person or over the phone.

c) Declining an invitation

It is always best to attend social events at work and with colleagues if you can. But what do you do if the event conflicts with other plans? Generally in North America, work-related and family conflicts are acceptable reasons to decline an invitation, but other personal conflicts are not.

For example, for an evening event:

Work conflicts that are usually acceptable reasons to decline an invitation:
i.   You have to finish a project at work that evening.
ii. You have to be at work early the next day for a specific reason.
iii. You have just returned from international travel and are really tired because of the change in time zone.

Family conflicts: The following statements may be reasons to decline an evening business event (or leave early). But one of them doesn't sound serious unless you explain it more completely. Which reason needs more explanation? [The answer appears at the end of this section.]
i.   You always call your parents at that time.
ii. Your spouse is sick at home.
iii. Your spouse has to get up very early the next morning to leave for a business trip.

iv. Babysitter problems: you are new to the area and don't have a sitter; you don't want to leave your children with a sitter; or the regular sitter isn't available at that time.

Which one is NOT a good reason to decline? (The answer appears on the last page of this unit.)

Personal or health issues that are acceptable reasons to decline an invitation include:

i. A strict medical or religious diet (for a dinner invitation).

ii. Health issues – they do not have to be explained.

Declining an invitation should always include giving a reason. Without a reason, the hosts might think you are declining because you don't like them.

d) SAMPLE RESPONSES:

Sara has received an invitation to dinner at a coworker's home but she doesn't want to go because she has a different life-style from a typical North American business person (for example, she follows a strict diet or she has family reasons that keep her at home). She can decline the invitation politely by **thanking and giving a reason:**

"Thank you for the invitation. I'd like to come, but…
- …I'm afraid my diet makes it impossible to eat out anywhere."
- …I have two kids and I'm not comfortable leaving them with a babysitter."
- …I have visitors from my home town, and I can't leave them alone."

In such cases, the host will probably try to offer to help so that Sara (and maybe her family too) can attend. Together, the host and Sara will try to find a solution.

If she absolutely can't (or doesn't want to) attend, then Sara should add another polite sentence or two to her response, for example:
- *"Thank you for the invitation. But I'm afraid that...* [reason]. *I'm sorry. Perhaps we can meet at another event sometime."*

Now she has made it clear that she is not going to attend. The host will likely not try very hard to change her mind.

If Sara does not want to talk about her reason to decline the invitation, she can say something like:
- *"Thanks for the invitation. I'd like to come, but I'm afraid I can't make it. Sorry about that."*

And the inviter will probably respond:
o   *"Oh, sorry to hear that. Maybe another time, then."*

ACTION:
1. In the office/class: give someone an appropriate, honest compliment today or invite them for a coffee/tea.

2. Consider volunteering or joining a sports group, perhaps with work colleagues. Both activities are healthy and, important and you can practice small talk as you meet new people with similar interests. In studies on happiness, psychologists and population researchers have found that volunteering makes life happier and more satisfying – all around the world.[33]

Answer to c. Family conflicts (pages 85-86):

i. *"I always call my parents"* needs more explanation. This reason is only OK if there is some very important, specific reason why the call must take place at the same time as the event you are invited to. If you are just planning to make your usual weekly phone call, many hosts (and bosses) would be disappointed that such a personal call is more important than their event.

Job Tip: The relationship between adults and their parents is not generally considered to be important enough to interrupt work functions in North America.

A new trend, however, is for companies to include parents, as well as children, in invitations to award ceremonies, take-your-family-to-work days, and staff holiday or summer parties.

UNIT 5
CUBICLE ETIQUETTE

There isn't much privacy in a cubicle office area. One in two office workers admits to having at least one bad habit that annoys their office colleagues. [34]

Answer the questions in this unit and find out **if you are a good cubicle neighbor**!

Key words: *cubicle, private/privacy, annoying, habit, odor, recycling, presenteeism, sick, ear buds*

There are 8 questions and 16 points in this unit.

Private offices are disappearing, replaced by open-concept offices. However, the latter are not ideal; research shows that in open-concept work spaces there are more absences due to sick days. As well, many employees don't like the distractions, noise, and lack of privacy. So now mixed spaces are becoming more common, with a variety of work areas: private, cubicle, and open space.[35]

1. Which of these <u>communication behaviors</u> is most annoying to the most employees in an open-concept office?

When a coworker often:

☐ **a. talks loudly**, on the phone or to other coworkers.

☐ **b. tells bad jokes.**

☐ **c. comes in late** and greets people cheerfully.

☐ **d. leaves a cell phone on** – and it rings for a long time.

Do you have any of these annoying habits?

2. What is the best way to let your workspace neighbor know that he/she is annoying you with that behavior?

☐ **a. Go to the supervisor** and complain.

☐ **b. Send an email to everybody**, reminding them not to annoy others.

☐ **c. Tell the annoying neighbor privately** that you would appreciate it if he/she changed that communication behavior.

☐ **d. Say loudly**, so that everybody can hear, "*Shut up!*"

3. Which one of these <u>environmental</u> <u>factors</u> annoys the most people in an open-concept area?

☐ **a. Smells** – people's food or body odor

☐ **b. The silence** when everybody just works at their computers

☐ **c. The temperature** of the room

☐ **d. Different recycling** habits (Some people carefully recycle paper, water bottles, etc., while others throw everything into the garbage.)

4. TRUE or FALSE? Your workspace isn't private, so it's OK for anybody who walks past your desk to read documents there.

☐ **a. TRUE.** The work space isn't private, so it's OK to read documents on people's desks.

☐ **b. FALSE.** The work space *is* private, so it's not acceptable to read other people's documents there.

☐ **c. TRUE and FALSE.** The work space isn't private but it's *not* OK to read documents there anyway.

5. SITUATION: Naomi likes jazz music. She says it makes her happy to listen to it at work. But she shares office space with Margaret and Jarmal, who don't like jazz. Margaret likes pop songs, and Jarmal prefers to work without music.

QUESTION: Can Naomi wear headphones or iPod ear-buds while she's working?

☐ **a. No, it's rude** to have headphones or ear-buds on. Naomi won't be able to hear her coworkers when they speak to her.

☐ **b. It's OK to wear them.** Naomi is then a happy employee and she doesn't annoy her coworkers.

☐ **c. It's OK to wear one ear-bud.** But Naomi should keep the other ear free so that she can hear her coworkers.

6. SITUATION: *Presenteeism* – when employees come to work even when they are sick – is a workplace problem, especially when people work closely together in a cubicle office.

People who cannot work from home have a hard choice to make when they are sick (not just have a cold). They have to choose between:
- staying home and not working

or
- going in to the office to support their team, coworkers or clients.

QUESTION: How many employees admit that they have gone to work sick? Take a guess:

☐ **a.** 74%   ☐ **b.** 57%   ☐ **c.** 33%   ☐ **d.** 9%

7. SITUATION: Su has a new job in Windsor. In her previous job she wore a suit. So in her new job she continues to wear a suit because it feels right to her. Her cubicle coworkers dress more casually, in sweaters and pants.

QUESTION: Which of the following statements probably represents what most of her coworkers think?

☐ **a.** They admire her because she looks professional.

☐ **b.** They think she wants to be a manager as quickly as possible. They also probably think she doesn't want to be friendly with coworkers at this level.

8. Is it OK for men to wear sandals to the office in the summer?

☐ **a.** Yes, it's OK to wear sandals in most office situations – with socks when the weather is cool and without socks when it's hot.

☐ **b.** Yes, it's generally OK to wear sandals or flip-flops to the office when the weather is hot.

☐ **c.** No, sandals don't look professional, so don't wear them to the office – unless the company allows *all* kinds of casual clothing, like shorts.

☐ **d.** Who cares?! Nobody notices anyway.

(There are notes about women's footwear, too, in the Answer section.)

UNIT 5. ANSWERS:

2 points for 1a, 2c, 3a, 4c, 5c, 6b, 6c, 7a, 8c
1 point for these answers: 1d, 3c, 5a, 5b

☐   ←   ←   ← WRITE YOUR SCORE HERE.

1. a [2 points]: Talking loudly is, for many, many people, the most annoying cubicle behavior. It is at the top of the list in many surveys. Often a colleague doesn't realize that he/she is using a loud voice. But 13 percent of office workers admit that they shout to coworkers over the cubicle walls sometimes – even though they know they shouldn't.[36] Others talk too loudly on the phone.

1. b [0 points]: **Telling bad jokes** can be annoying but this doesn't happen as often as loud talking. And telling *good* jokes can help keep the office staff happy!

1. c [0 points]: Generally, a **cheerful "Good morning"** is welcome at work. In fact, many people (77% of an international survey) are very annoyed if they are <u>not</u> greeted in the morning![37] But it could be annoying if you are coming in <u>late</u> and greeting everybody regularly.

1. d [1 point]: Leaving a cell phone on that then rings and rings and rings… is the Number 2 annoying habit in many offices. Turn the sound off your cell phone while you are at work, please.

MANAGING ANNOYING BEHAVIOR

2. a [0 points]: **Complaining to the supervisor** will only annoy the supervisor! Coworkers should be able to find some solution to this relatively small problem themselves.

2. b [0 points]: **An email to everybody** might not influence annoying coworkers if they don't realize that they are loud. It's not very effective. As well, it's not your duty to remind everybody of proper behavior; that is the supervisor's or manager's job.

2. c [2 points]: **Talk to the annoying neighbor privately.** As mentioned above (**1. a**), many times the loud talker doesn't know he/she has that bad habit. Avoid saying *"You should not"* (like a parent or teacher), which implies that you know more than other people (see page 107). Just explain briefly and in a friendly way that you and others can hear his/her conversations. Usually a short conversation is enough.

2. d [0 points]: **"Shut up!"** is a rude expression. Don't use it at work. And if you shout it out to everybody, then you are even more annoying than your loud coworker!

3. a [2 points]: **Smells** are the Number 1 environmental problem among coworkers.[38] Smelly lunches and body odors make a person unpopular. Unfortunately, it's not possible to take action against smells – you cannot close your nose like your eyes and ears! But North Americans don't like to discuss such personal issues. So if odors are a problem, it might be best to have an all-staff meeting to discuss them, or ask a manager to help make some rules for everyone.

SMELLS

Cultural Note: Body odor and scents

North Americans are extremely sensitive to body odor and are embarrassed if they meet anyone who has it.

Many people:

- wear deodorant – they might even apply deodorant more than once a day, especially in hot weather or hot rooms or after a gym workout.

- take a 7-8 minute shower[39] every day; many also wash their hair daily, especially women.

- wash their clothes after wearing them once, just to be sure they're fresh, even though it isn't usually necessary.

- chew gum or take a breath-cleaning candy after lunch so that their breath doesn't smell bad.

Body odor makes a person unpopular. But because it's so embarrassing, nobody likes to say anything about it.

While deodorant use is expected in North America, perfume is not. In fact, some workplaces are now "scent-free." (Review page 16.)

THE CUBICLE ENVIRONMENT

People like different dishes, and food habits can be strong. If colleagues bring their spicy lunches to work and eat at their desks, there will be odors. Food smells are often even a problem when there is a kitchen – if the door is left open.

Cultural Note: It's my lunch

When North American employees have lunch, over half of them eat alone.[40] Even if they sit with others, they usually don't plan to share their food. They just eat their own lunch. In the same way, if a group goes out to a restaurant, they order individual meals. This sometimes surprises colleagues from other cultures, where it is rude not to offer to share food at the table. (Exceptions are Asian restaurants or where a menu offers a meal for several people.)

---

3. b [0 points]: **Silence** is rarely a problem in "the cubicle jungle"! Some people may prefer music to silence; in most offices they can wear a headphone or use ear buds to listen privately. [See Question **6** below.]

3. c [1 point]: Yes, **room temperature** can affect people differently. But in most cases, you can take personal action. You can wear warmer clothes if it's too cold, or wear lighter ones if it's too warm in the room.

Room temperature should be managed by a supervisor if it is a health problem or affecting most employees' happiness and productivity.

MORE ANNOYING OFFICE BEHAVIORS

3. d [0 points]: **Recycling habits** can differ among coworkers. In worst-case scenarios, people who strongly support recycling watch everybody else to make sure they follow city and company policies. They are sometimes called "eco-bullies" or the "green police" ("green" refers to environmentally friendly procedures/policies).

4. Most cubicle workers want to feel that their work space belongs to them and is therefore private. Many people put family photos, etc., on their cube walls to personalize the space. However, see the answers below:

4. a [0 points]: While it is TRUE that your cubicle isn't private, that doesn't mean that others are allowed to read your papers there.

4. b [0 points]. Wrong answer.

4. c [2 points]: TRUE *and* FALSE: The work space isn't private but it's not OK to read documents at coworkers' desks. Your North American coworkers will be annoyed if you come by their cubicles and read their papers or computer screens.[41] They will also be unhappy if staff members take supplies, such as stapler or pens, off their desk. However, it is actually their responsibility to put away or cover documents that should not be available to others.

In some companies, employees no longer have their own desks. Instead, they sign up for any appropriate space (cubicle or office) when they arrive at work. Their paper files are in an assigned drawer or locker. This system is called "hot desks" or "hotelling." With work space for only about 75% of the staff, it works well when 25-35% of the employees are away every day, visiting clients, etc.

MUSIC WHILE YOU WORK?

5. a [1 point]: Many people agree that earbud use is rude. **It isn't polite** if a coworker regularly uses headphones to escape from talking to others in the office. If Jarmal and Margaret feel that they can't talk to Naomi when she wears ear buds, then she shouldn't be allowed to wear them.

For safety too, **employees must be able to hear** when someone speaks to them. For these reasons some companies don't allow them; however, in a lot of other workplaces, they are OK, and about one third of American workers have them on at work (across all industries). [42]

5. b [1 point]: Many people work better with music, especially when they are doing routine tasks, although for difficult mental work, music can be a distraction. When people can choose their favorite music, regardless of their coworkers, they are likely to be in a good mood. (But Naomi should not sing along with her jazz!) So, even though some employees don't like it, it has recently become **more common and more acceptable to wear headphones or ear buds** in the office. In large, open concept offices, they give the worker some privacy and personal "space."

5. c [2 points]: Wearing one ear bud (instead of both) can be a good solution. Some people, like Jarmal, don't like to hear music while they work; so it is good etiquette – and good ear health – not to play the music so loudly that coworkers can hear it. Good manners also mean taking the ear-bud out during a conversation, face-to-face as well as on the phone.

HEALTH AND SICK DAYS

6. a, d [0 points]: Guess again about **presenteeism**.

6. b [2 points]: 57%. In the past, according to many surveys, about 50-60% of employees admitted they had **gone in to the office sick**.[43] Their most common reasons:
- Workload: they had too much work to do.
- They didn't want colleagues to think they were lazy.

On the other hand, some stayed home: one in five employees said they didn't want to infect their colleagues. Most workers prefer that sick colleagues and their germs stay home.

Presenteeism and significantly lower productivity also occur when workers have not slept enough at night.

Sick Days and other absences around the world

The average American full-time employee is absent from work because of illness or disability about 6 days each year. Canadian workers with full-time jobs usually receive pay for 6-10 "Sick Days" per year and stay home for 7 days (13 for unionized workers).[44] Generally, in workplaces with a good work environment employees are absent less often. Employers have the right to require a doctor's note to prove illness, but many bosses do not insist on one for a 1-2 day absence.

Internationally, managers' tolerance for absence varies. A recent study reported that, within a six-month period, employees in large companies were absent (for any reason) 8 days in India, 5 in Pakistan, 3 in Nigeria, 2 in Mexico, and 1½ in Japan and the U.S.[45] The absences might not be due to illness: another study showed that about one-third of Americans occasionally call in sick when they are not ill.[46] Around the world, notable absence levels occur during World Cup soccer matches.

DRESS FOR THE JOB

6. c [2 points]: 33%. More sick workers stay home **during flu season** but still one in three employees in surveys said they went to work feeling unwell. Some stayed home for about a week but came back when they might still have carried the flu.

7. For a review of **business dress**, see page 17.

7. a [2 points]: While it's understandable that Su might overdress (dress too formally) on her first day at work, she should adapt to the unspoken dress code and company culture. If Su wears a suit every day while her colleagues dress less formally, they will probably **not admire** her. Women have a wide range of clothing choices, so if someone chooses to overdress, "coworkers have a tendency to view this with suspicion ...not respect" according to fashion expert Amy Verner.[47]

7. b [0 points]: Su's coworkers might have any of these negative thoughts. If they do, she might not be an effective team member if her coworkers don't like her. And unfortunately, Su might not make friends at work for a while – until the others get to know her personally. This situation won't be a problem if Su and her colleagues **talk about it** and get to know each other's opinions and feelings about office clothing.

> *True story: When an employee in a casual-dress non-profit agency came to work wearing a blazer one day, her coworkers asked, half-jokingly, "Oh, have you got a job interview today? You want to leave us?"*

SANDALS IN THE OFFICE?

8. a [0 points]: No. Men with any fashion sense at all **do not wear socks with sandals**. A study in British Columbia, on Canada's west coast, showed that 69 percent of all people, and an even higher percentage of women, don't like to see men wearing socks with sandals.[48] This custom is in contrast to some other cultures.

Job Tip: Sock Fashion

Most women and men in Canada and the United States dislike socks with sandals. They use a variety of adjectives to describe the look, such as: *uncool* or *unfashionable*.

When you wear socks with shoes, the socks should have about the same color as your pants. Men: white socks are not for the office (unless you're wearing white pants).

For women the question is often whether to wear stockings or not. Stockings are required in formal offices. Some companies have a spoken or written rule that women cannot have bare legs.

If you aren't sure what is proper in your office, observe your coworkers and managers or ask the HR manager.

---

8. b [0 points]: Like **sandals, flip-flops** are not dressy; in this illustration the woman is wearing weekend casual clothes. Flip-flops can be dangerous in workplaces with machinery, ladders or uneven floors, so most employers don't allow them.

ADVISING COWORKERS ON PERSONAL CHOICES

8. c [2 points]: Opinions vary on sandals. Every summer, newspapers from Florida to San Francisco to Toronto have articles about wearing sandals to work. For example, a *Toronto Star* survey asked readers: "Is it appropriate for men to wear sandals to work during the summer?" Readers' answers were split almost 50-50 but a tiny majority (52%) said "No."[49]

8. d [0 points]: **Maybe you don't care what you wear**, but lots of people notice clothing! That's why there are a lot of news and magazine articles about it. Review the answers above – and then, of course, make your own choices, within the dress code of your office.

Cultural Note: Giving soft advice to coworkers

North Americans respect one another's personal space and privacy, so they don't usually like to give negative personal advice to colleagues. While they might give fashion tips to their friends, they don't often correct fashion or language mistakes of their coworkers. And while there might be discussions on general news, for example remedies for the current flu, most people don't give substantial advice on personal issues of a colleague like health, weight or pregnancy. Unlike in some cultures where giving advice is seen as being helpful, in the North American workplace it is often perceived as **negative criticism**[50] so it is avoided.

If you have to give advice to a colleague (at your level), use some softening expressions like *Maybe you could* or *I think maybe* or *I'm afraid that might not...* Avoid *should*, which implies superiority, unless you are a boss, who can give orders

---

HOW TO SAY IT: POLITE REQUESTS

Cultural Note: Corporate hierarchies

In many countries, companies have a formal seniority structure and many manager ranks. Junior staff don't often start conversations with senior staff nor ask for favors. When they do speak up, junior staff use special politeness with higher-ranked managers.

In North America, companies have fewer ranks and don't pay so much attention to formal seniority. For instance, most people call each other by their first names. However, even here, when employees ask for help or for a favor, they are careful to choose an appropriate level of formality.

Teamwork is very common in project management. Team members make requests for, and respond to, help or feedback. When office workers ask for help or for a favor, they choose among expressions from a range of formality levels. Their language depends on:
- the rank of the person they're speaking to
- the difficulty of the help requested.

New employees, who might need to ask a lot of questions, should be sure to be polite, so that they don't annoy coworkers.

Do you have a good sense of the right level of politeness for simple and complicated requests?

1. Very informal, direct language is appropriate for a very simple request or question:
- Got a red pen I can borrow for a minute?
- Where's the key?

The first request is so informal that it isn't even a complete sentence. (*Have you...* is missing from the question.) This is fine for casual conversations.

There are several ways to ask a question more politely, for example:

2. Use polite vocabulary like "could" and "please" – these are neutral but polite words – for a request that isn't very difficult:
- <u>Could</u> *you lend me your key to the file cabinet downstairs for a minute?*
- <u>Could</u> *I borrow your stapler,* <u>please</u>*?*
- <u>Could</u> *we meet tomorrow to discuss this further?*

3. Make the question longer by starting with an indirect introduction. A question without an introductory expression (like *"Where is the key?"*) can sound abrupt. One way to make a direct question more polite is to add an introduction. The longer question shows politeness and seriousness.

3. a. If you are not already in a conversation, introduce your question or request gently by starting with *"Excuse me."* This is appropriate for more serious situations, for example:
- <u>*Excuse me*</u>, *could I use your color printer?*
- <u>*Excuse me*</u>, *could I ask you a couple of questions?*

3. b. Introduce the question with *"Do you know...?"* or *Do you think you could...?* The answer to the question is *Yes* or *No*. It allows the other person to say *"Sorry, I don't/ can't..."* without losing too much face. These are polite requests – for something that can be a little bit difficult:

- *Do you know where the key is?*
- *Do you think you could help me clean up after the lunch meeting tomorrow?*
  This is a request that asks the teammate for his/her time and labour.

B-i-g requests are helped by asking l-o-n-g questions.

4. A very polite request – for something difficult that takes quite a bit of time or money – needs a longer introduction:

- *Do you think you could possibly give us an extension – an extra half-day – on this project?*
- *Would it be at all possible to give us an extension...*
  This is a big request. But note that this isn't a personal request about someone's free time; it's a company matter.

5. A formal, very polite, personal request – for something that involves a lot of money, time (especially personal time), work or privilege – requires a very long introduction. The long expressions *"I hope you don't mind my asking"* and *"I was wondering if it might be at all possible"* are appropriate for an unusual or complicated favor, usually from an employee of lower position or rank to a manager or supervisor. They are also appropriate expressions to use, separately or together, in a difficult situation if you almost expect a negative reply:

- *I hope you don't mind my asking, but I was wondering if it might be possible to take a couple of days off starting tomorrow.*
  This request is difficult because it involves other employees, who must work harder while you are away. It is not likely to be successful if no reason is given, even though the language is very polite.

To get a positive reply to polite questions and requests, **it's a good idea to add the reason, why you need help.** People are usually friendlier when they understand why their help is needed.

ACTION:

1. What **practical advice** did you learn? Review this chapter and list a few tips that are important to you:

_____

_____

_____

2. Research some policies of your company or school (or local library or employment centre), such as:
- Recycling rules
- Lunch room and cooking practices
- Presenteeism and sick day policies
- Office / Work space privacy expectations
- Headphone rules
- Dress code

Job Tip: Get advice on your first presentation.

If your new job requires giving presentations in meetings or to clients: As a new employee, you might need advice on your first presentation to help you to meet company expectations. The Manager might not give very many details and will probably expect you to develop it quite independently.

Most people have trouble rating their listening and public speaking skills and judge them higher in effectiveness than their actual performance, according to American research.[51] So it could be useful to practice with a trusted colleague or mentor to get some objective feedback.

If English is not your first language, ask a colleague to give you honest feedback on your language skills because it is difficult to assess them yourself. The Centre for Canadian Language Benchmarks in Canada says of immigrants with English as a second language:

"One of the challenges faced by a number of programs working with internationally trained individuals at CLB 7-10 [intermediate to low advanced language levels] is participants' denial that language is an issue or barrier."[52]

As long as your language is understandable to others – grammar, vocabulary, accent (light accents in English are not a problem in this century of global business) – and you can make your topic exciting, you can be a good candidate to give a presentation.

If any employee has never made a presentation in a meeting or to a client: Good companies encourage staff to develop all their skills. The employee could be offered coaching or a training course.

UNIT 6
MEETINGS AND TEAMWORK

In this chapter you will find answers to questions like:

- How important is punctuality for meetings?

- Is it OK to check my smart phone during a meeting?

- What can you expect from good teammates at work?

Are you a good team member? Answer the following questions.

Key words: *punctual, enthusiastic, take initiative, team responsibility, accomplishments, charity, following the agenda, action items*

There are 8 questions and 16 points in this unit.

1. SITUATION: You have an internal team meeting at 1:00.

QUESTION: What time should you arrive?

☐ **a.** 1:00.

☐ **b.** About ten minutes before 1:00.

☐ **c.** It's not very important exactly when you arrive – it's natural that busy people are sometimes delayed.

Cultural Note: The twelve-hour clock

Canadians and Americans use a 12-hour clock:
- Midnight to noon hours are 12:00 – 11:59 **a.m.**
- Noon to midnight hours are 12:00 – 11:59 **p.m.** (instead of 12:00 – 23:59 in the 24-hour clock)

---

2. SITUATION: You have an appointment for a job interview (a special kind of meeting) at 11:00.

QUESTION: What time should you arrive?

☐ **a.** 11:00.

☐ **b.** About ten minutes before 11:00.

☐ **c.** About twenty minutes before 11:00.

☐ **d.** It's not very important exactly when you arrive - it's natural that people sometimes have trouble finding a place they have never been before.

Noon is 12:00 p.m. and midnight is 12:00 a.m.

The abbreviations "a.m." and "p.m." are seldom used except for transportation or work schedules and some formal invitations.

---

3. Do you know what your "body language" (nonverbal behavior) says to other people?

SITUATION: You are at a meeting of 12 people from different departments of your company, sitting around a table.

QUESTION: Which of the following behaviors are OK? Check as many as you want.

During the meeting you can:

☐ **a. yawn** – if you hide it behind your hand.

☐ **b. blow your nose** into a handkerchief or tissue.

☐ **c. burp** – if you've just had something good to eat.

☐ **d. take notes** to refer to later.

☐ **e. quietly take your shoes off** under the table.

☐ **f. lean back in your chair and close your eyes** in order to concentrate on the speaker.

☐ **g. check your phone** for messages.

4. SITUATION: At a team meeting, an American colleague begins to talk about a solution to a problem.

You understand quickly, agree, and have some ideas to add, so you should:

[Choose one best answer.]

☐ **a.** wait respectfully until the colleague has finished talking and the **team leader has responded.** Then ask if you can add some supporting ideas.

☐ **b.** wait until the colleague has finished talking and there has been a **short silence** so that everyone can consider what he/she said. Then offer to add some ideas to the discussion.

☐ **c.** when the **colleague has finished talking,** add your ideas.

☐ **d.** show your agreement by beginning to talk as soon as you understand what the colleague is saying, **even if he/she isn't quite finished.**

☐ **e.** **choose your response** depending on whether you are a junior member of the team or an experienced senior member. A junior member should wait until the team leader asks for an opinion, then respond with ideas. A senior member can begin to express his/her ideas as soon as the colleague's solution is clear.

5-6. TRUE or FALSE?

5. In a team meeting, anybody can disagree with the leader if there is an important matter to get right.

☐ **a.** Generally TRUE ☐ **b.** Generally FALSE

6. Team members have individual responsibilities. A team leader expects each member to be responsible for the success or failure of his/her own tasks. If the project succeeds, the leader might praise the whole team but also praises (at a meeting or privately) any individuals who had exceptional accomplishments.

☐ **a.** Generally TRUE ☐ **b.** Generally FALSE

7. How important are formal meetings, attended by more than one level of staff?

☐ **a.** Formal meetings are **very important.** That's where most company decisions are made.

☐ **b.** Formal meetings often are **not very important.** The real work is done outside of meetings

8. SITUATION: a charity committee meeting. Many companies have committees that organize company or community activities for United Way or other charity organizations. Employees often attend committee meetings and charity activities during their paid work time.

QUESTION: If your company has some activities to support charities, **do you (does everybody) <u>have to</u> participate?**

☐ **a. Yes.** It's a company event so you must participate, whether activities are during work hours or after work.

☐ **b.** You have to participate if it is during work time but not if it is in your free time.

☐ **c. No,** you don't have to participate. You can choose to be active or not.

UNIT 6. ANSWERS:

2 points for 1b, 2b, 3d, 4c, 5a, 6a, 7b, 8c
1 point for 4a, 4e, 8b
½ point for 1a, 2c, 7a
Subtract **one point** for 3a, 3c, 3e!

☐   ←   ←   ← WRITE YOUR SCORE HERE.

1. a [½ **point**]: Normally most people are too busy to arrive ten minutes early to an internal team meeting, and that is not expected. But observe your company culture: in some workplaces that might be an unwritten rule, so that team members can chat (face-to-face).

1. b [**2 points**]: Good, **you are on time.**

1. c [0 points]: Wrong answer. Usually employees are considered **late** to an internal meeting after about four minutes (1:04). The business world is time-sensitive. Send the meeting chairperson a message if you realize you are not going to make it on time.

2. a [1 **point**]: If you arrive at the interviewer's office exactly at the stated time, you are punctual – but **are you ready?** There is no time for reflecting on your self-introduction, etc.

2. b [**2 points**]: Advantages of an early arrival to a job interview:
- You can sit and think or relax, maybe find a restroom.
- You can see people and the office atmosphere.
- You impress the interviewer with your reliability.

MEETING ETIQUETTE

2. c [½ point]: Don't be too early, for example twenty minutes or more![53] It looks as if you are desperate for the job (you will take anything). Interviewers would rather think that you are enthusiastic about this particular job. In addition, it can make both you and the office staff nervous if you are waiting and watching for a long time.

2. d [0 points]: **Wrong answer.** Job applicants are expected to be early or on time. Being late to an interview is at the top of the list of behaviors that annoy employers[54], so be punctual! You can help yourself by locating the place the day before so that you know how long it will take you to get there.

3. The only widely accepted meeting behavior is d, take notes.

3. a [*minus* ½ point!]: **Yawn – No.** Even if you hide an open-mouthed yawn behind your hand, people will know you are yawning. In North America, a yawn means you are bored or the meeting isn't interesting enough to keep you awake. Don't open your mouth to yawn.

3. b [½ point]: **Blow your nose – Yes...if** you use a tissue. (Never wipe your nose with your bare hand.) Turn your head away and give your nose a quick, quiet wipe. In fact, most people would much rather see you wipe your nose than hear you sniffing constantly, which is considered very annoying. However, if you blow your nose very loudly, leave the table to do it.

MORE ON MEETING ETIQUETTE

3. c [*minus* ½ point!]: **Burp – No**. Although it might be OK in some cultures, in North America burping isn't polite, even at or after a good meal. Adults don't burp in public. (Children sometimes burp in public for fun and to annoy the adults.) As well, brush your teeth or take a breath-candy after a spicy meal because many people are very sensitive to anything noisy or smelly about the body.

3. d [2 points]: **Take notes – Yes**. It's OK, and even smart, to take notes for later. If technical terms are new to you or English isn't your native language, you can help yourself by following the agenda. An exception is a meeting that is announced as confidential.

3. e [*minus* ½ point!]: **Take your shoes off – No**. This is only done when relaxing at home; it isn't appropriate at work. And there is the danger of odors (again!).
3. f [0 points]: **Lean back, close your eyes – No**. If you close your eyes at a meeting, it will look as if the meeting is boring you and making you sleepy – whether you lean back in your chair or not. (And if you put your hands behind your head, you will look arrogant to some people.) This doesn't mean that you have to sit formally straight all the time, but show that you are awake. The speakers will be looking around at everyone and you should make eye contact with them too.

> **Job Tip: Eye contact**, which establishes trust between people, is very important in business meetings. This is especially true for women, who tend to focus on their discussion partners' eyes to get feedback when talking or making a presentation.[55]

PAYING ATTENTION AT MEETINGS

3. g [0 points]: Check phone – No, but... many people admit that they do it in some meetings. Among managers in a 2014 poll, 61 percent said that it isn't unusual for professionals to check emails during a meeting; but only four percent of them approve of this behavior and almost half say that it is never OK.[56] Younger people are generally more accepting of this behavior among themselves.

You might be taking notes on your cell phone, or say you are (instead of checking for email, etc.); but if your attention is directed at your smart phone, somebody will notice – unless there is a busy discussion going on. And if there's a discussion, you should be part of it; people will notice, too, if you don't say anything. See **f** above regarding the importance of eye contact.

For Question 4, answers will vary. They depend on the company culture and the team leader's and your own personalities. However, there are certain expectations about appropriate meeting behavior – see the answers below.

4. a [1 point]: Wait respectfully until...the team leader has responded. Then ask... This answer is OK but timid (not brave or strong). It doesn't make you look like a very self-confident, energetic person. See **4. c** for more effective meeting participation styles.

123

RESPONDING TO OTHERS

4. b [0 points]: **Respond after a short silence.**
This will be a good response *only if* the company culture follows this pattern. In general, this behavior isn't typical of North American meetings. Many Canadians and Americans don't feel comfortable with silence. Rather than being respectful, **silence** after someone's suggestion is often negative, meaning that nobody can think of anything good to say about it!

4. c [2 points]: **Add your ideas** without much hesitation.
This is the best answer. It shows that:
1) you have listened carefully
2) you have ideas and are not afraid to express them
3) you are a quick thinker and take initiative.
You also support your colleague when you quickly agree.

4. d [0 points]: **Begin talking... even if the colleague isn't quite finished yet.** No. This kind of enthusiasm is acceptable in many cultures, but in North America, especially in Canada, speaking up before someone else has finished talking is interrupting. Interrupting is bad manners and rude, even if you do it while agreeing with your colleague. The colleague wants to finish making a point. After that, other people can take the initiative and speak up with praise or comments. (See also Unit 9 #1.)

4. e [1 point]: **Choose your response depending on whether you are junior or senior.**
In some companies, this is the appropriate way to behave at a meeting. But in most companies in North America, new ideas and quick thinkers are valued, and *all* employees are encouraged to speak up.[57]

RESPONSIBILITIES IN A TEAM

Job Tip for getting ahead: Employees who stay quiet at meetings will not usually be promoted because they don't act like future leaders.

---

5. a [2 points]: Generally TRUE. *In a team meeting, anybody can disagree with the leader....* but be respectful. Every team member has a responsibility to contribute to team efforts. If you have experience that is valuable, you should mention it, even if you disagree with someone.

But if you are new to the company, it is best not to disagree too often or too loudly too soon! Coworkers don't like people who suggest a lot of changes in their work procedures without fully experiencing the work flow in the company first.

Cultural Note: Men and women may lead differently

Many studies have shown that men and women have rather different leadership styles. Women are often more willing to make suggestions, consult others, and include everyone in discussion. They sometimes talk about the situation (or even tell an illustrative story) before getting to the point. Men are often more direct, dominant when they lead, and more challenging than women.

---

6. a [2 points]: Generally TRUE. *...the leader praises individual team members...* Teamwork is praised and individual accomplishments are too. They are often mentioned when a project has been successfully concluded, since each individual's tasks and responsibilities are known.

ARE ALL THESE MEETINGS NECESSARY?

6. a continued: An employee who has received praise, or an award, can mention the accomplishment and the praise later to advantage, for example:

- at a performance review
- in a job interview.

7. a [½ point]: There are too many meetings, and they often **aren't very productive**, in the opinion of most office workers and many managers. In recent years, some companies have developed a policy that **no** meetings can be scheduled for Fridays (or another workday) so that employees can work with fewer interruptions.

7. b [2 points]: A professor of management explains: "In most organizations, only about **ten percent of business** takes place in formal meetings and events. The real process of making decisions, gathering support, developing opinions, etc., happens before or after the meeting."[58] The time around meetings includes building relationships through socializing and networking. It is especially important for new employees to participate in such informal discussion opportunities so that they can be part of the decision-making.

8. a [0 points]: You **aren't required** to participate in charity activities. See **c** below.

8. b [1 point]: About half the working population likes to do charity work on the job. A big city newspaper asked this question online[59]; over seventeen thousand people responded.

VOLUNTEERING FOR A CHARITY COMMITTEE

- 51% said they *like* to support charity programs at work.
- 36% said they prefer to donate to charities privately.
- 13% didn't like to do charity activities at work.

A survey by the accounting firm Deloitte & Touche found that 62 percent of young working people (18-26 years old) "want to work for companies that provide volunteer opportunities in the not-for-profit world."[60]

8. c [2 points]: You don't have to participate. For charity activities you can just say "No, thank you" if you don't want to participate. But it's best to give a reason too.
A good example of an acceptable reason: you already support a charity privately. Companies try not to pressure employees to join in such activities at work.

Charity committees usually include people from different company levels and areas, without many managers, so that a lot of views are represented.
There are advantages to volunteering on such a committee. You can:
- meet new people.
- network with managers that you don't see otherwise.
- try new roles and responsibilities, such as leading meetings, showing leadership potential.

◆

Now go to page 192 and enter your scores for Part 2 (Units 4-6) in the chart. Add them up and see how good your business soft skills were when you started this section. Now, after reading all the solutions, you know more about soft skills for getting along in the office!

HOW TO SAY IT: MOVING MEETINGS ALONG

Well-organized meetings follow an agenda. The leader, or Chair, needs to ensure that the meeting ends with **results – decisions made or action items** assigned – within the set time frame. So participants are asked to follow meeting etiquette by focussing on the agenda points and not discussing other matters.

Be aware of language: English-speakers often use idioms in business talk. Colleagues or international partners who speak other languages might not understand them. Some of the most common business idioms are expressions about talking[61] and moving meetings along.

The following are important idiomatic verbs to be aware of, including their meaning and an example of how they are used in a meeting.

to go through something, to go over something
✓   to explain something thoroughly, step by step
*"Let's start by **going through/over** the action items from the last meeting."*

to bring up
✓   to direct attention to, or start a <u>new</u> subject/topic
*"He **brought up** his accomplishments throughout the year at his annual review meeting."*

to point out
✓   to direct attention to something that nobody else has mentioned
*"May I **point out** that these figures don't add up correctly?"*
to get to the point

✓ to say something directly

*"**Get to the point**, tell me what you want. I don't want to guess."*

to get back to

✓ to return to a topic (or respond to someone's comment)

*"We'll **get back to** your point in a moment, but first we have to discuss something else."*

to go on

✓ to continue, to proceed

*"**Go on**, explain your idea further."*

*They **went on** to the next point of the agenda.*

ACTION:

As you **participate in meetings** at work or school or on a volunteer committee, observe the body language and spoken language of the participants. Listen for vocabulary, particularly how speakers move from one topic to the next and how they use soft skills to agree and disagree with each other. By listening for language with a specific function, you can become more aware of your own communication skills.

(If you have no access to a real meeting, watch an American movie, TV show or online video with a business theme. However, these are media of dramatic entertainment, so they might feature far more confrontational than cooperative behavior.)

Part 3

SOFT SKILLS FOR WORKING WITH THE BOSS

UNIT 7

SUPPORTING YOUR BOSS

In this unit you will find answers to issues like:

- How to know when a polite boss is actually giving an order

- Whether to get your boss a gift at Christmas or year end

- What to do if a project isn't ready by the deadline

 Key words: *deadline, problem-solving, 'green' (environmentally responsible), social event, commitment, ethical, blame, apology*

There are 8 questions and 16 points in this unit.

1. Good bosses use polite language even when they give orders. However, they expect staff to understand the difference between a polite order and a question.

Decide which of the following is a polite <u>order</u> from the boss, and which is just a <u>question</u>.

a. "Could you please give me that report by 5:00 today?"

☐ Order   ☐ Question

b. "Can you come to my office for a few minutes?"

☐ Order   ☐ Question

c. "Would anybody like the air conditioner turned down?"

☐ Order   ☐ Question

d. "See you at the company charity event this weekend?"

☐ Order   ☐ Question

2. SITUATION: Your job starts at 9:00 in the morning.

QUESTION: How important is punctuality - being ready to start work on time?

□ **a.** You should always be ready to start work on time (8:55 - 9:05) or early, never late.

□ **b.** Life is difficult sometimes. It's natural that you will be late to work once a month or so, with a good reason.

□ **c.** Punctuality every day isn't really important. What's important is that you do every project or task well and finish it on time.

3. SITUATION: Your boss asks you to complete a project by tomorrow but you know that it will take about three days to do it.

QUESTION: What should you do?

☐ **a.** Nobody really expects that the project will be ready tomorrow. Tell your boss what he/she wants to hear, then **work at a normal speed** to get it done in two to three days.

☐ **b.** Tell your boss the project will be ready tomorrow. **Then work all night like crazy**, asking everybody to help, even though you probably can't be successful.

☐ **c.** The boss wants to hear the truth, so say that the project will take about three days and **it is impossible to finish** by tomorrow.

☐ **d.** Explain the truth: that the project will take about three days. Then **offer to get one part finished by tomorrow** if that will help him/her.

4. SITUATION: You are working on a project as team leader and see that it won't be finished by the deadline.

QUESTION: Should you tell the project manager?

☐ **a. No, just keep working.** It's not your job to report this. It's the project manager's job to explain to the senior managers why it's not finished.

☐ **b. No, and make sure the project manager doesn't find out** beforehand. When the deadline comes, you can explain why it's not finished, if necessary.

☐ **c. Yes,** tell the project manager as soon as you know about the delay. Don't wait for him/her to ask. **Explain the problems and suggest solutions.**

☐ **d. Yes,** tell the project manager about the delay, **complaining** that other people or departments have not done their part to meet the deadline.

5. SITUATION: Zak wrote a report on cost-saving and emailed it to his boss Betty yesterday. He hasn't received a reply yet. He knows Betty is busier than usual this week. But he is scheduled to go on vacation in three days, and he doesn't want her to lose his report or forget about it while he's away.

QUESTION: Zak wonders how to bring his report to Betty's attention. What would you advise?

☐ **a.** He should plan to go to Betty's office two or three times a day and remind her of his upcoming vacation and the report until she reads it. Since she has the report in her email, she can easily look it up when he reminds her.

☐ **b.** He shouldn't bother Betty when she is busy in her office but should mention the report when he sees her in the hallway, elevator, cafeteria, etc.

☐ **c.** He should go to Betty's office just to ask her if she has any questions about the main points of his report. Then he can also send an email suggesting a short meeting before he leaves on vacation.

6. SITUATION: Your company writes in its advertisements that it is 'green,' environmentally responsible. That means that it is actively reducing negative effects on the environment that come from producing its goods and services.

Now your boss is sending you and two coworkers to a business meeting in a city about five hours' drive from your office. The boss tells you to book flights with the company's travel agent.

One of your coworkers would like to drive and doesn't want to fly.

The other one thinks that you should all take the train to the meeting because it is the most environmentally responsible.

QUESTION: What should you do?

☐ **a.** Take the plane, as the boss said.

☐ **b.** Agree to go with your driving coworker so that at least two people will be in the car.

☐ **c.** Agree to take the train with your 'green' coworker.

☐ **d.** Talk to the boss about going with one of your coworkers. Then decide.

☐ **e.** None of the above. You have your own idea:

_____

7. SITUATION: Many companies have one or more big social events during the year, where all the employees can enjoy a party together, for example, a picnic or barbecue in the summer, an awards dinner, or a Christmas or Holiday Party in December. Everyone is invited to the event. Attendance at the party is sometimes considered work time.

QUESTION: Do you really have to go to a company party?

☐ **a. Yes.** It's a company event so you should go.

☐ **b.** You only have to go if it's during work time but not if it's in your free time.

☐ **c. No,** you don't have to go. You can choose to go or not. You can work (if the party is during work time) or go home instead of attending the party.

8. SITUATION: It has been a good year for you at this company. Now it's November and the staff are beginning to talk about the annual company party in December. Everybody will bring one gift and receive one. You plan to go to the party and take a gift, too.

QUESTION: Should you buy a present for the boss, as thanks for the good year, in addition to the gift for the party?
(More than one answer might be good, but choose just one.)

☐ **a. Yes**, a very nice gift. You want to impress the boss.

☐ **b. Yes, but** only a small one, $20-$30. It's a nice thing to do.

☐ **c.** You should **join your coworkers** if they buy a gift for the boss as a group but shouldn't give a present just from you alone.

☐ **d. No**, employees shouldn't buy a gift for the boss.

UNIT 7. ANSWERS:

2 points for 2a, 2b, 3d, 4c, 5c, 6d, 7a, 8c, 8d
1 point for 2c, 6e, 8b
½ point each for 1a 'Order', 1b 'Order', 1c 'Question', 1d 'Question', and for 3b, 3c, 4d, 6c

☐   ←   ←   ← WRITE YOUR SCORE HERE.

1. a: 1 point for 'Order' [0 points for 'Question']. The boss uses polite language (*Could you*) and a question form, but this is not a question or suggestion. The boss expects action. You have to have the report finished today by 5:00; and "by" means "at that time or before."

1. b: 1 point for 'Order' [0 points for 'Question']. The boss expects you to come immediately or very soon, not in 10-15 minutes or when you have finished what you are doing.

1. c: 1 point for 'Question' [0 points for 'Order']. This is just a question, not an order. It doesn't mean that the boss wants to turn down the cold air.
If the air-conditioner bothered the boss, the question would be: *Does anybody **else** want the air-conditioner turned down?*

1. d: 1 point for 'Question' [0 points for 'Order'].
Participating in charity events is optional [review Unit 6, Question 8], so this isn't an order. You should answer the question honestly (don't say yes if you're not going to go) – and give a reason if you will not attend.

"ON TIME" AND "TOMORROW"

2. a [2 points]: Daily punctuality, arriving on time at the beginning of the day or shift, is usually expected in office jobs. And 60 percent of employees support their managers and team by regularly getting to work on time.[62] However, some managers don't require it – see **b** and **c**.

2. b [2 points]: One in four employees admit that they arrive **late at least once a month**. Traffic is a major reason. The majority of managers (about 60 percent) accept that. They might react with understanding or concern when someone comes in late, asking, *"Traffic bad today?"* or *"Is everything OK?"*

Only 10 percent of managers are so strict that they consider firing an employee who is late occasionally. If they see someone arriving late, they might say, *"Don't let it happen again or I'll have to make a note in your file."*

2. c [1 point] Thirty percent of managers say that daily punctuality isn't as important as **good quality work that is finished on time**. Managers' tolerance towards punctuality reflects the trend to flexi-time and telecommuting (working from home) as well as the growing number of consultant and contract positions. There are now about 18 million such jobs in the United States.[63] (This situation is often called the "gig economy," where "gig" means a contract, freelance, or temporary job. Examples of gig workers are many Uber drivers or a musician with contracts at different venues.)

3. Your attitude towards deadlines, and how you communicate it, is very important! Punctuality in business deals is a serious matter. *"I'll get it done tomorrow"* means it <u>will</u> be done tomorrow, not three or even two days later. So it is best to stick to the facts when talking about deadlines with your boss.

141

DEADLINES

3. a [0 points]: The boss will not like this plan to say Yes when you're thinking No. (It is sometimes unfairly stereotyped as "Third World attitude.") North American business people want the "hard facts" so that they do not disappoint the partners who are waiting for the project.

3. b [½ point]: This is a good option only if you think working all night can be successful. However, if the project still isn't finished by the next day, you have lost the goodwill of the boss as well as the people who stayed up to help. Next time you ask, they might stay away because they don't trust your judgment.

3. c [½ point]: This answer is true but not the best because you have only said "no." You haven't shown your problem-solving skills. Managers are always looking for staff who support them by actively helping them to solve their problems.

3. d [2 points]: The boss wants the facts, so explain the truth, with a positive statement like "I'm working on it" – even if the boss gets angry. At least then the boss can make other plans, like extending the deadline or adding more staff to the project. Offer to deliver one part finished by tomorrow, too, if that will help.

4. a and b [0 points for each]: **If you simply do not meet your commitment**, the project manager will lose face and be in trouble with his/her boss and the client. The manager will think you can't handle responsibility well, too, which will certainly be noted in your performance evaluation.

SUPPORTING YOUR BUSY BOSS OR MANAGER

4. c [2 points]: If you are working on a project and realize that you will not get it finished by the deadline, **don't wait for the project manager to ask you** about it. It is expected that you tell him/her about the expected delay in advance. And if you add your ideas for solutions, it shows that you handle responsibility well. Early reporting supports the manager by allowing him/her to make alternative plans and save the project.

4. d [½ point]: Blaming others isn't the best way to explain problems. And most good bosses don't emphasize blame very much. It's more important to find out what went wrong and then ensure that the same problem doesn't happen again in the future.

5. a [0 points]: Don't nag. Zak will annoy Betty if he continually, for example twice a day, stops by her office. Betty is very busy. It is smarter for Zak to <u>ask</u> than to remind Betty; that's good etiquette – see **c** below.

5. b [0 points]: Don't ask when the boss is busy with other things. It is not effective for Zak to ask Betty in the hallway, when she's busy thinking about the next task that she's walking to, or in the lunch room when she's relaxing or socializing. She can't respond properly.

5. c [2 points]: Asking if she has questions about the main points of his report has the advantage of narrowing the focus of Zak's question. It gives Betty the opportunity to focus on and ask about those main points if she hasn't yet read the report (and has time to listen).

CONSIDERING YOUR OPTIONS

5. c [continued]: It also gives Zak the opportunity to tell Betty the main points. In both cases, Betty gets the most important information, whether she has time to read the whole report or not. If Zak wrote his report well, it includes the main points at the beginning, in an **Executive Summary**. A busy boss can scan them quickly and easily.

In addition, it's smart to communicate in two ways: speaking face-to-face as well as emailing, since there are different advantages to each. Some bosses react better to one way than another, especially when they're busy. Asking for an appointment – at Betty's convenience – may be better done by email so that Betty can check her schedule. Zak then also has a record of his attempts to connect with Betty.

6. Ethical travel choices: A newspaper column "Business Ethics" posed a similar question about travel choices in *The Globe and Mail*, a national newspaper in Canada. Ten representative responses from readers were published. Their advice agreed with answers **a, c** and **d**.[64]

6. a [2 points]: Do what the boss says. Almost half the letter-writers (four out of ten) thought that it was most important to support the boss' suggestion. The boss might want staff to save time by traveling fast, and in the plane you and your coworkers could talk. Most of these writers didn't suggest talking to their boss about other choices. But a few suggested that they could talk about the ethics of train travel at some good opportunity in the future.

DO WHAT THE BOSS SAYS?

6. b [0 points]: **Go with your colleague in the car.** No writers agreed with the colleague who wanted to ignore the boss and drive, although one reader wrote that car travel is the cheapest when several people travel together.

6. c [½ point]: **Go with your colleague in the train.** This is environmentally friendly, but you should discuss it with the boss first. Your green colleague should not change company policy based only on his/her own feelings. In this case, when you talk with your boss, you can point out the company's advertising message as well as the benefits of train travel. (Support: It is not just good for the environment, but also the cost is lower than flying. Train travel provides a quiet time for relaxing or catching up on notes with your coworkers, just as the plane does. In addition, there are few security line-ups in train stations, and often no long taxi rides to downtown, so taking the train can be efficient.)

6. d [2 points]: **Talk with the boss first. Then decide.** Sixty percent of the letter-writers did not want to follow the boss blindly, without question (see answer **6.a**). These responders probably have workplaces where they can make suggestions to their boss. In fact, many employees feel comfortable talking with a manager and even offering a different opinion, especially if it can be supported by facts, numbers and ethics. Seeing your interest, the boss might change his/her mind. This wouldn't be unusual in the average North American office, where employees are generally allowed to make suggestions.

COMPANY OUTINGS

6. e [1 point] if you wrote a good suggestion: Two other possible solutions are:
- use an environmentally friendly hybrid car
- hold the meeting as a video- or teleconference, the greenest way to meet across long distances

If you make a suggestion, you can impress the boss. But you also need facts, dollar amounts and ethics to support your arguments.

7. a [2 points]: Yes, if you care about your career in that company, **you have to go to the company parties.** Good bosses plan a company party as an enjoyable event that they are happy to spend money on. It is often organized by staff from all departments in order to include the interests of everybody. Therefore, it is impolite to refuse to go. Support your company: 41 percent of senior managers expect it[65] and etiquette experts and agree.

7. b and **c** [0 points]: People will notice if you are **absent** from the yearly party. If the company tradition is to attend, some people will think that you are not a friendly person or that you don't like your colleagues if you are absent. If you had the wrong answer to this question, you need to study this book!

Review "Declining an invitation" (Unit 4, pages 85-86) if you really cannot or don't want to attend, and send an appropriate RSVP.

COMPANY PARTIES

There are many good reasons to attend the annual
company party. It's good for networking, meeting people:

- Talk to colleagues informally (small talk), to get to
  know them better.
- Make personal contact with staff members from
  other departments – that improves communication
  when you work together on projects later.
- Meet the boss informally. That will help him/her to
  remember you. (But don't follow the boss around,
  trying to impress – that's annoying.)
- Have a good time!

If spouses/partners are invited, make the party enjoyable
for them. Don't worry too much about the rules for
introductions – it's not a formal situation. Couples usually
begin their socializing together. They might separate later
to speak with different people (rarely to dance with other
people).

8. a [0 points]: If you give the boss **an expensive gift** but
no other staff member does, then that looks bad. It looks
as if you want special notice. Your colleagues won't like
that behavior and probably the boss won't like it either.

8. b [**1 point**]: If there's a company tradition of not giving
any presents, then your gift could look bad. However, if
you have had a good year working with your boss, or you
have a particular reason to want to thank him/her, then
a small gift is OK. It shouldn't be anything that is too
personal to show around the office.

A GIFT FOR THE BOSS?

8. b continued: You can give a common gift item, such as candy or a specialty coffee or tea, or it can relate to the boss's hobby, like golf balls or a gift certificate to a book store. But don't give a coffee mug – the boss probably has a hundred from past years!

> *True story*: *A preschool teacher routinely receives gifts from parents of her pupils on the last day of school before Christmas break: chocolates, soap, mugs, coffee shop gift certificates (although she is a tea drinker), etc. And every Christmas she "regifts" most of them to others because she has so many.*

8. c [2 points]: Yes, join your coworkers if they give a group gift. You can still write a personal note, too. The organizer of the group should consult (not dictate to) everyone about the gift item and the amount of staff contributions to it.

8. d [2 points]: Since employees earn less money than their bosses, they are not expected to give individual gifts. In fact, many bosses ask staff not to give them anything at all.

> **Job Tip: Instead of a gift, why not write a note** of thanks or appreciation? A handwritten note is rare these days, and can be very meaningful, especially to the "boss who has everything." You could thank them for mentorship, patience, understanding, the opportunities he/she allowed you, etc.

HOW TO SAY IT: CONTRIBUTING POSITIVELY

Consider this situation:

Ann: *My computer is down this morning.*
Lee: *Oh no! How could that happen? We'll never finish by the deadline now! And the boss will blame all of us.*
Jae: *Good thing you emailed me the latest version of our report last night. We can work from that. Let's get on it.*

Lee is being negative, emphasizing the bad news and looking backwards for fault and forwards only to blame. Unfortunately, this kind of negativity and unhappiness can spread easily to everyone else in the office. Jae is being positive and constructive, looking forward and ready to continue working toward the goal. It's much easier to work in a positive atmosphere, and a lot more is accomplished.

1. Use positive statements to be a good team member – and to show the boss that you are doing your job well:

- *Good thing...*
- *We're on schedule.*
- *I'm on top of it.*
- *I'm on it.*
- *We're on a roll.*
- *You can count on me/us.*

Although company cultures vary, generally **managers need staff that can be proactive**, give well-supported suggestions, and help them solve their problems. They don't need staff who complain about, or blame, others.

2. Avoid the "blame game":

Both managers and employees should avoid the negativity of blaming.

a. Use impersonal words like "it" or things, instead of naming names:

Not: _Norma didn't use enough details._
Better: _It would_ (or _might) be better to add more details._

Not: _Tom and I didn't finish the project on time._
Better: _The project wasn't finished on time._

b. Don't set up a win-lose situation with _you_ vs. _me_, but instead work constructively together as _we_, and look forward, not backward:

Not: _You told me to do it that way._
Better: _Those were our instructions._

Not: _I knew your plan wouldn't work. It never worked before. You should have done it my way. Now we're behind schedule._
Better: _We're behind schedule. How can we move forward quickly now? Let's get together on this._

c. If you made a mistake, admit it, apologize once, and help to move forward:

Not: _Sorry, sorry, sorry. I ruined it._
Better: _Sorry. I didn't realize that. Next time I'll be sure to take that into account._

Not: *It's all my fault. I'm so sorry!*
Better: *My mistake, <u>sorry</u>. I think <u>we can correct it by</u>...*

Just like polite questions, apologies should be longer for more serious issues.

d. Don't use loaded words like *blame* and *fault*, even for yourself:

Not: *Who is to <u>blame</u> here?*
Better: *Let's figure out how to avoid this problem in the future.*

Not: *Sorry! It's all my <u>fault</u>. I didn't understand.*
Better: *There must be a <u>misunderstanding</u> here. Let's see if we can pinpoint the problem and then fix it and move on.*

Tip: If one person "didn't understand," it's usually a communication problem involving two people: the person who instructs or explains as well as the listener/ receiver.

ACTION:

1. Give at least one positive, supportive reply to a manager, coworker, student or neighbor today!

2. Review these ways to support a boss. Suggest more.

_____

_____

151

UNIT 8
UNDERSTANDING FEEDBACK AND CRITICISM

This unit provides answers to questions like:

- When the boss gives you feedback, how should you respond?

- How can you give polite criticism?

- What are some good ways to respond to a sarcastic comment?

- Does cultural background affect the kind of feedback one gives, or the reaction to feedback?

 Best responses to questions in this unit will vary in real life, depending on company culture and managing styles and expectations.

 Key words: *constructive feedback, feedback sandwich, criticism, objection, save face, sarcasm, tone (of voice), defensive, deal*

There are 8 quiz questions and 16 points in this unit. For many questions, more than one response may be acceptable.

PART 1. FEEDBACK

Feedback from the boss

Although there are some differences among managers' styles of feedback, generally they agree on the following points:
- Feedback is about performance on the job. Criticism that attacks someone's personal life is unacceptable.
- Feedback that is too general, not specific, isn't very helpful.
- **Constructive feedback**, that names a problem, shows that improvement is possible, and suggests a solution, is best.

Many (but not all) managers give a '**feedback sandwich**.' That means they have three points when they talk to their employee:
- First they say something good to show they value the employee's contribution to the company.
- Then they discuss something that the employee needs to improve, a negative comment, often with a solution.
- Then they finish with praise for something the employee does well, to keep his/her confidence up.

They believe that it is easier for a person to change behavior when there is both positive and negative motivation.

The employee needs to make sure that he/she understands the negative comment in the middle so that he/she can improve in that area.

1. SITUATION: You are an Office Manager. You are not pleased that one of the staff has been coming to work late.

QUESTION: How can you give <u>constructive feedback</u>?

☐ **a.** *"You never come on time. You can't get your work done that way."*

☐ **b.** *"Sometimes people have to come to work late, but that's not very helpful for the team, especially when they are working on a big project."*

☐ **c.** *"Your team is working on a big project. But you have come late three times this week. The team needs you to start work on time from now on."*

☐ **d.** *"You're lazy. And your attitude doesn't seem to be improving."*

☐ **e.** Answers **a, b**, and **c** above.

2. SITUATION: You are an employee receiving feedback from your boss.

QUESTION: Which of the following statements could introduce the middle of a feedback sandwich? In other words, you need to pay attention if you hear something like this because it is probably the beginning of a negative feedback statement.

☐ **a.** *"Your work is pretty good, considering you just joined the staff a couple of weeks ago. Now we need to bring you up to speed on ..."*

☐ **b.** *"I'd like to see you take some initiative."*

☐ **c.** *"You probably didn't check with your team leader before you made that proposal, did you?"*

☐ **d.** all of the above

3. As an employee, what is the proper way to react to your manager's feedback?

☐ **a.** This is a time for listening quietly, not talking. Don't say anything.

☐ **b.** Listen carefully and ask about anything that you're not sure you understood.

☐ **c.** Listen and respond to every negative comment.

☐ **d.** Respond by explaining why you are a good, hard-working employee, not like some of your co-workers.

☐ **e.** All of the above are OK. It just depends on your personality.

4. SITUATION: Giving feedback to your manager.

The manager of your department has prepared a sales presentation for a client. Because you have dealt with that client, he/she emails you the presentation and asks for your comments and corrections in a few sentences. You find a weakness in it: it doesn't include enough back-up data.

QUESTION: How do you begin your comments? Choose the best of the three following suggestions:

☐ **a.** "I believe your presentation has a few faults. For starters, your data fail to support your case. You have to use data from the last five-ten years rather than just two..."

☐ **b.** "Thank you very much for the privilege of helping you with your presentation. I'm impressed by your arguments. However, you must increase the data to cover the last five to ten years..."

☐ **c.** "As you requested, this is a quick, brief analysis. The base data, figures from the last two years, do not necessarily show the full range of our advantages. Our client would likely prefer data based on a longer period. It may work well if we include the last five-ten years..."

PART 2. CRITICISM

5. SITUATION: At a meeting, a colleague is describing a solution to a problem. You have some objections to the solution. Because of your experience on the job, you know that plan won't work.

QUESTION: What should you say?
(More than one answer might be possible but choose just one.)

☐ **a.** *"I'm afraid there may be some issues with that idea."* [Continue with your objection.]

☐ **b.** *"Have you considered...?"* [Continue with your objection.]

☐ **c.** *"If we put this plan in place, how would we deal with...?"* [Continue with your objection.]

☐ **d.** *"Your plan won't work. Let me tell you why. My experience shows..."* [Continue with your objection.]

☐ **e.** You shouldn't say anything unless someone asks you. It is the responsibility of the leader of the meeting to ask for other opinions as needed.

6. SITUATION: Your boss gave you instructions on how to do a task and you followed those instructions. When the task is finished, the results are wrong. The boss asks you to explain why you gave him/her the wrong results.

QUESTION: How do you answer?

☐ **a.** *"You gave me the instructions yourself and I just followed them."*

☐ **b.** *"It was suggested that I do it that way."*

☐ **c.** *"I have no idea why the results are wrong."*

☐ **d.** *"Oh, I think someone in the other team gave me some wrong information."*

☐ **e.** *"It's all my fault. I'm so sorry! I guess I didn't understand your directions."*

159

7. SITUATION: Cathy is a good employee who works hard. However, today she is 15 minutes late for a meeting led by her boss. Her boss is not pleased with her lateness. He/She is a bad boss, who uses sarcasm in belittling comments to embarrass people.

QUESTION: Which of the following comments is sarcastic?

☐ **a.** *"Well, you honor us with your presence, Miss Too-Busy-For-Meetings? Glad you can finally join us."*

☐ **b.** *"I hear you have a busy schedule today. Come on in. We're talking about..."*

☐ **c.** *"You're late."*

☐ **d.** The boss says nothing but frowns at Cathy.

8. QUESTION: If the boss is sarcastic to her, what kind of reply should Cathy give?

☐ **a.** A sarcastic or nasty reply, such as: *"I've never yet missed anything important in the first 15 minutes of your meetings."*

☐ **b.** A reply to defend herself, such as: *"Well, if you had announced the meeting earlier in the week, I would have had time to plan for it in my schedule."*

☐ **c.** An apology, such as: *"Sorry! I'm so sorry to be late! It's my fault. I couldn't plan my day very effectively."*

☐ **d.** No reply is necessary. Cathy should just quietly sit down and show that she is ready to join the team's work.

UNIT 8. ANSWERS:

2 points for 1c, 2d, 3b, 4c, 5a, 5b, 5c, 6b
1 point for 2a, 2b, 2c, 6a

☐   ←   ←   ← WRITE YOUR SCORE HERE.

1. a [0 points]: *"You **never** come on time..."* This generalizes too much with the word "never." The comment doesn't show the employee how to improve; it's not helpful, just negative.

1. b [0 points]: *"Sometimes **people** have to come to work late..."* This is too general, not specific; it doesn't mention specific behavior of the employee at all.

1. c [2 points]: *"Your team is working on a big project. But you have come late three times this week. The team needs you to start work on time from now on."* **This is constructive feedback. It is specific and gives a solution, how job performance can be improved.** The problem (the negative meaning) in this case is that the employee isn't helping the team enough. Specific details: "late three times this week." Solution: "start work on time" now.
Note: In constructive feedback, sometimes the manager asks the employee for his/her own ideas on how to improve performance so they can problem-solve together.

1. d [0 points]: *"**You're lazy**. And your attitude doesn't seem to be improving."* This is a personal attack. It doesn't see any hope for improvement in the employee's behavior. The feedback is unhelpful, unprofessional, and unacceptable.

1. e [0 points]: Wrong answer. See above.

Cultural Note: Giving feedback in multicultural offices

In every office, there are some people who are more sensitive to criticism than others. In multicultural offices, where a manager or employee has work experience from another culture, criticism and feedback can be especially confusing. The way managers give their employees feedback can be strongly influenced by work culture. Cultural experts Lionel Laroche and Don Rutherford explain this in their book *Recruiting, Retaining, and Promoting Culturally Different Employees*[66]:

"Misunderstandings often arise when giver and receiver do not have the same cultural background. Different cultures have different scales for interpreting feedback...

On average, people from the Middle East, Eastern Europe, Israel, Germany, the Netherlands, Belgium, France and Italy tend to be less sensitive to feedback than North Americans...For example, North American listeners often interpret comments made by their Polish teammates as harsh criticism when, in fact, they were intended to be only slightly negative...

On average, people who come from Latin America or East Asia tend to be more sensitive to feedback than North Americans. In this case, mild criticisms or jokes made by North Americans may be taken very seriously by Mexicans or Chinese, more seriously than they were intended."

Among North Americans, business people in Canada give softer feedback than those in the United States.

GENTLE NEGATIVE FEEDBACK

2. a [1 point]: *"Your work is pretty good, considering you just joined the staff a couple of weeks ago. Now we need to bring you up to speed on ..."* This subtle comment could be Canadian negative feedback. It starts with two qualifiers that show that it isn't completely positive: *pretty* and *considering*. The expression *pretty good* usually means it is <u>not</u> excellent or very good but only so-so and some improvement is needed. [However, *"Pretty good!"* has a range of meanings. The true meaning depends on the speaker's intonation (voice melody) in a particular situation. Some people mean it more positively than others.]

Then, by referring to your behavior in the first weeks, the boss points out that you are still learning about the company and need to make some changes. *"bring you up to speed on..."* will introduce some specific advice, the middle of the feedback sandwich. That will explain where you are not yet meeting company expectations and why your work is only *pretty* good right now.

2. b [1 point]: *"I'd like to see you take some initiative."* This is criticism. Many managers complain that newcomers don't take risks or take the initiative at work. For example, they don't join new projects if the project isn't directly in their field. From the manager's point of view, this means that the new employee isn't interested in promotion but is happy doing only what he/she does now.

> **Job Tip: Employees who want to rise to the next level** are expected to develop their skills by taking on extra responsibility <u>before</u> a promotion. Managers promote people who have already proven they can handle higher-level tasks.[67]

REACTING TO FEEDBACK

2. c [1 point]: *"You probably didn't check with your team leader before you made that proposal, did you?"* The boss is advising you to check with your team leader next time. This is the opposite of **b**, the case where the employee didn't take initiative. In this case, the employee jumped too far. Note that the boss's feedback, a negative question, is not harsh.

2. d [2 points]: *All of the above* are negative comments. **See each point above** if you didn't choose this answer.

3. a [0 points]: *This is a time for listening quietly, not talking.* ***Don't say anything.*** **Wrong answer.** It is important that you show that you understand the feedback. See sample responses in the other answers (**b, c**).

3. b [2 points]: *Listen carefully and ask* *about anything that you're not sure about.* You will learn what the boss expects if you listen carefully. He/She is helping you to fulfill company expectations, and develop your skills.

- Ask questions if you aren't sure whether comments were negative, for example, a direct question like *"What improvement would you like to see in the future?"*
- If there is a specific criticism that was mentioned, but you aren't sure about future expectations, you can ask *"How can I improve this?"*
- Your boss might ask you for your own suggestions. If you can think of a change that you know you can make, then your solution will probably be successful.

POSITIVE AND NEGATIVE RESPONSES TO FEEDBACK

3. c [0 points]: *respond to every negative comment.* **No,** don't argue with your manager's point of view. Don't try to show why you were right, or at least partly right, for each point. If you defend yourself at every comment, that sounds like arguing. Your job is to understand and follow company expectations. When the manager is finished, you can respond with a comment such as:

- *"I didn't realize I was doing that* [specific behavior]. *Have there been any other times when I did that?"*
- *"I didn't realize that my work style was annoying other people."*
- *"Could we discuss more about why you think that?"*

3. d [0 points]: *explaining why you are a good... employee,* **not like some of your coworkers.** This answer is also defensive. Don't blame or criticize others; it's unprofessional and irrelevant. The feedback is for and about you only.

3. e [0 points]: **No,** it does not *just* **depend on your personality** *which way you react.* Your boss expects you to react professionally. Only response **3. b** is a positive, professional reaction.

Job Tip: Senior staff need you to understand and follow company expectations. Have respect for your manager during a feedback session; he/she is telling you how to improve your behavior so that you can keep your job. The ability to accept feedback and change behavior afterwards is very important. New employees who react badly to feedback, or can't change their work habits or performance, often lose their job. This is a more common reason for dismissal than lack of technical skills.[68]

WATCH YOUR LANGUAGE IN COMMENTS TO THE BOSS

4. Writing comments to the boss: The three email responses in this question all address the task; they all provide the same critical comment about the manager's data. The difference is in the tone of the message. Just as we can have a friendly, angry, or arrogant tone of voice in speaking, so can our writing show feelings. Business communication professors have the following advice for employees who have to write reports[69]:

4. a [0 points]: This email wins no points because it **blames the manager** (*"you"*) for the bad presentation: *your data fail*. Its first sentence contains negative words (*faults, fail*) and the writer sounds like a teacher giving instructions: *you must....* The phrase *For starters* says that there are more criticisms after this one. Altogether, the manager will feel as if the employee is accusing him/her instead of helping. This writer needs more soft skills!

4. b [0 points]: This email begins with language that is **too formal and flattering** (*the privilege...I'm impressed ...*). Perhaps the employee was trying to form a feedback sandwich, starting with a positive comment; however, the opening sentence doesn't sound true or honest when followed by the negative comment about the data. The criticism, using the strong verb *must*, **sounds like an order** or a teacher's instructions (like in **a**).

The two tones of this comment are not appropriate for a lower-level staff member to send to a manager. This writer needs better soft skills, too.

DISAGREEING POLITELY

4. c [2 points]: This email begins with neutral language (*this is …*). Instead of using strong or absolute terms, the writer uses **softer vocabulary and lots of qualifying words**: *not necessarily, full range, likely, prefer, may work well…*

As well, the writer uses *we* and *our,* **showing that he/she feels like being on one team** with the manager, rather than the opposing terms *I* and *you.* In addition, the writer **gives a reason** for suggesting the longer term for data (*…show the full range of our advantages*) in a way that emphasizes strengths of the company and benefits for the client. This email is helpful and constructive (doesn't blame anybody) and supports the manager.

PART 2. CRITICISM

5. a [2 points]: *"I'm afraid there may be some issues with that idea."* This objection or concern uses polite language in three ways: First, it begins with a polite expression ("I'm afraid…"). Second, it is indirect, only suggesting ("may be") that some problems exist without aggressively stating it. Third, it uses diplomatic vocabulary: "issues" instead of the negative word "problems."

5. b [2 points if you say it in a friendly voice]: *"Have you considered…?"* This objection is OK because it is a question. It shows respect for the colleague by allowing the colleague to explain. He/she can thus save face in front of the people at the meeting. He/she can either give his/her own answer or open up the question for general discussion by everybody.

POLITE AND LESS POLITE OBJECTIONS

5. c [2 points]: *"If we put this plan in place, how would we deal with...?"* Like **b** above, this is a question for discussion. It asks "How" and doesn't say No directly. And questions with "If" and "would" are indirect, not aggressive. During the discussion, people will have a chance to say their points of view. The group will see whether your objection is really a problem or not and an effective decision can perhaps be made in the meeting.

5. d [0 points]: *"Your plan won't work. Let me tell you why. My experience shows..."* The short sentences here are very direct and can sound aggressive. The vocabulary is not diplomatic because it sets up opposition between *you* and *me*: *you* have a bad plan, so I will correct you because *my experience* is good.

Your colleague won't feel respected or happy with this response; in fact, he/she will feel like a child whose parent or teacher is lecturing. This kind of response will not make friends for you at the meeting; it doesn't make you a good team player, either.

Compare the language here with the gentle advice to coworkers suggested in UNIT 5 CUBICLE ETIQUETTE.

5. e [0 points]: 'It is the responsibility of the leader of the meeting to ask for other opinions': Wrong answer – review UNIT 6 MEETINGS AND TEAMWORK. **Every employee has the responsibility** to contribute to team efforts. If you have experience that is valuable, contribute it; just avoid undiplomatic words like those in **d** above.

THE BLAME GAME

6. Most good managers don't react mainly by blaming people; so don't start **"the blame game"** yourself.

6. a [1 point]: *"You gave me instructions."* This is true but not good soft skills because it so clearly **blames the boss**: His/her bad instructions led to the wrong results.

If the boss is open to honest feedback, great! Otherwise, this answer might be considered rude. The boss might become angry and the conversation might not be productive after that.

6. b [2 points]: *"It was suggested that..."* This statement **doesn't blame** anyone directly, so the boss can save face.

6. c [0 points]: *"I don't know."* This answer avoids a clear statement but it also **makes you look stupid**. However, in a job website poll, twenty percent of employees admitted they used that lie sometime at work.[70]

6. d [0 points]: *"...someone in the other team gave me some wrong information."* **This answer is not ethical**. This lie is a dangerous statement because the boss could easily check it with the leader of the other team. However, five percent of two thousand web survey responders said they have once blamed a colleague for something in order to look good to the boss.[71]

6. e [0 points]: *"It's all my fault. Sorry..."* **Saying Sorry** a lot, apologizing for something that you did wrong, should rarely be necessary. Women seem to do it more than men[72] and Canadians more than Americans.

SARCASM FROM THE BOSS

6. e continued: Although it can be polite to start with *"maybe I misunderstood,"* **don't take all the blame** on yourself. It is seen as being weak – not polite – especially among men in the American business world.

7. a [2 points]: Sarcasm includes exaggeration. In this comment the expression *honors us* and the adverb *finally* are exaggerations; the verb *honors* is used for very important people such as heads of governments. As well, using an unreal name, *"Miss Too-Busy-For-Meetings,"* is childish and embarrassing for Cathy. It sounds as if Cathy thinks she is too important to come to the boss' meeting.

Cultural Note: Men and women and sarcasm

Men and women may react differently to sarcasm. Belittling and embarrassing comments annoy women a lot.[73] On the other hand, it's not uncommon for men to make sarcastic jokes and comments about each other, for example in sports, so they are more used to them.

---

7. b [0 points]: Tone of voice is important here. This comment is probably **polite**, not over-exaggerated. The boss recognizes that Cathy has a busy work day. In this situation, Cathy has a good boss.
(However, the first sentence <u>could</u> be sarcastic <u>if</u> Cathy was clearly having a lazy day and not working hard.)

7. c [0 points]: This short comment isn't polite but **it's true**. People are usually considered late if they arrive more than about four minutes after the beginning of a meeting. Since it isn't an exaggeration (it's true), this comment isn't sarcastic.

REACTING TO SARCASM

7. d [0 points]: Sarcasm applies to something spoken. If **the boss says nothing**, then he/she isn't sarcastic.

8. a [0 points]: Give a **sarcastic reply.** Some people, especially men, feel they must hit back if they are treated unkindly. However, the boss is a person of respect – even if he/she isn't nice. It's dangerous to be sarcastic with your boss. (Note: in some companies there is a culture of embarrassing people. In that case, an employees who want to advance to management might think they have to make sarcastic remarks, too. That would be an exceptional case.)

This situation is about a woman. Studies show that angry women are more disliked than angry men.[74]

8. b [0 points]: **A defensive reply.** Don't blame the boss, especially not in front of other people! This isn't a wise comment to make, even if it is true.
[For more about blaming at work, review Unit 7 HOW TO SAY IT.]

8. c [0 points]: **A long apology.** Although you might think it's good to apologize (especially if you are a woman), be careful not to blame yourself too much. This apology is too much. People will begin to believe you aren't a good worker if you blame yourself for every little problem. This is especially important for business women to note.[75] In addition, this comment is so long that it interrupts the meeting – see **8. d.** Although a long apology is too much, a short one, just *"Sorry,"* would be appropriate. Cathy could also apologize for not having sent a note: *"Sorry, I should have let you know."*

HUMOR AND EMOTIONAL REACTIONS

8. d [2 points]: In all cases, whether the boss makes a sarcastic or a kind comment when she comes in, **Cathy should stay calm.** She should not make a long comment in reply. A discussion of her lateness would just interrupt the team's discussion. She should either just sit down quietly or say something positive, like "*Sorry to interrupt. Please continue the discussion.*" If the boss continues to be sarcastic, Cathy can leave the meeting calmly.[76]

> **Tip: A pleasant, funny comment** can also be a good response. Humor, a good soft skill, can make a difficult situation less stressful.

After the meeting: Cathy could try to talk with the boss in private. This can be difficult, especially because the boss has a higher position than she does. However, it can produce good results. Cathy can explain that she is happy to work hard if everybody is respectful of each other. She can mention what the boss said that she found disrespectful so there is no doubt about what she means. To do this well, she needs to be assertive, i.e. have a confident and positive attitude. As well, she needs to be respectful. [More about assertiveness in Unit 9.]

> *True story: A manager and the company president had different work styles. The manager liked to keep project files and products that she was working on on her desk. The president asked her to follow company policy and clear her desk every night, saying, "You know what they say: a cluttered desk means a cluttered mind." The manager replied, "Well, then, what does an empty desk mean?" She knew the president understood humor. To be supportive, from then on she also tried harder to keeper desk clear.*

HOW TO SAY IT: PHRASES FOR NEGOTIATING

Have you ever thought about the number of ways we use the word "*deal*," casually or seriously, in business?
- o *It's a deal.*
- o *a deal-breaker*
- o *a done deal*
- o *a good/bad deal*
- o *to deal with it*
- o *dealer*

etc. Negotiations, or deals, are the core of business.

Here are some other important phrases in business and:
- ✓ their meaning
- • an example of how they are used
- ❖ **their significance in negotiation strategies**.

Some expressions are also used for feedback.

the bottom line
- ✓ the final result, often the final financial result
- • The bottom line is that we both want to come to an agreement.
- ❖ **Know the result you want**: Are you going for a win-win situation, will you be satisfied with a compromise, or do you want to crush the other side? (The latter is not a good idea if you're negotiating with your boss!)

at issue
- ✓ the problem, what we need to discuss
- • At issue here is the high cost of doing business abroad; that's our main concern.
- ❖ **Be clear about the subject** of the negotiation. Don't let distractions or emotions change your goal.

174

open to ideas
✓ flexible and willing to consider new ideas
• *We're prepared to listen to your proposal. We are always open to new ideas.*
❖ **Open minds create open doors – and increase opportunities** for successful results.

not up to par [informal, rarely used in the positive sense]
✓ not good enough, not equal to our standards
• The records show that your reports are not up to par yet. Deal with that first and then we can talk.
❖ **Be ready to give reasons for rejecting** the other side's arguments and support your own negotiating position. Talk about issues; know your facts and the other side's weaknesses – but avoid personal criticisms.

to be straight with you, to be blunt
✓ to tell you the truth, speak very directly, not gently
• *I'll be straight with you: Your offer isn't what I hoped for. To be blunt, I've had better offers.*
❖ These two expressions are better than the similar expression "*to be honest.*" The latter implies that you might not always be honest!
❖ Successful business negotiators often **take charge, lead the negotiations**, rather than follow: Act like a winner and you will be seen as a winner.

We'll see. [informal]
✓ I'm not convinced yet. I'm not promising to take action now. Future events will show us.
• So you want more? We'll see. Let's look at your numbers again next month and then discuss it.

❖ **The manager's mind is still open.** From a manager to an employee, *"We'll see"* does not mean *Yes*. On the other hand, it doesn't automatically mean *No* either. The manager might suggest the next step for the negotiation. At that time the employee needs to provide more supporting facts to prove his/her point.

I realize

✓ I understand or recognize – and appreciate
• <u>I realize</u> that you may want some time to study this, but we really need your response by Friday.
❖ These are very helpful words in negotiations and an expression of good soft skills. *"I realize"* can show that you are trying to **be fair and see the other side's point of view.** Then they will likely also try to understand your points. Result: less conflict.

ACTION:

1. At work/In class: Look again at some feedback you have received from your boss/instructor. Does it follow the classic feedback sandwich formula?

2. Use the expression *"I realize"* in your next negotiation or discussion to show understanding of another point of view. Note the reaction of the discussion partner: Does he/she then change to a softer approach or appear to be more relaxed?

UNIT 9
SOFT SKILLS FOR TOUGH SITUATIONS: ASSERTIVENESS

Office life often requires a certain amount of assertiveness. **Assertive** behavior means standing up for your rights and point of view, rather than either letting someone "walk all over you" or, on the other hand, aggressively starting a fight. For example, if Cathy chooses to talk to her boss to explain that his/her sarcasm is hurtful to her (UNIT 8, question 8), she is acting assertively.

Here are several situations in which being assertive may help you to reach your goal, starting with fair discussion strategies:

- Avoiding interruptions in a meeting
- Taking an after-hours work phone call from the boss
- Asking for a raise
- Asking for unscheduled time off

 Key words: *assertive, raise, track, make up time*

This unit has 4 questions and 16 points!

1. SITUATION: A Manager has called a meeting to discuss the current project. Marc has an idea that he would like to explain completely without interruptions. Sophia, one of his colleagues, often interrupts people in meetings.

QUESTION: When Marc starts speaking, what can he do if Sophia tries to interrupt him? (More than one answer might be possible, but select just one.)

☐ **a.** Say *"Go ahead, Sophia. Ladies first."* Let Sophia interrupt. Marc can continue with his idea after she has finished speaking.

☐ **b.** Keep talking, loudly. Sophia will have to stop talking if Marc is louder.

☐ **c.** If Sophia interrupts him, then Marc can interrupt her. *"Excuse me, if I could just finish..."*

☐ **d.** If Sophia interrupts him, it's OK for Marc to show that he is annoyed. *"Sophia, please be quiet until I'm finished."*

2. SITUATION: You are eating dinner after a long day at work. You get a phone call from your boss. He/She wants to make sure you are ready for a big meeting tomorrow.

QUESTION: What do you do? (More than one answer might be good but choose just one.)

☐ **a.** You stop eating dinner and give your full attention to the phone call.

☐ **b.** You multitask. While you are talking with your boss, you secretly continue eating.

☐ **c.** You give your boss a short, polite answer and tell him/her that you are in the middle of eating dinner. You ask if you can call back in an hour or at another convenient time.

☐ **d.** You tell your boss that now isn't a good time to talk because you are in the middle of eating dinner with your family.

3. SITUATION: Davon is in Sales. He has been talking with a potential client for a several weeks. Today the client company signed a contract and became a new customer. Davon feels great. His confidence is so high that he wants to go to his boss right now and ask for a raise, based on his current success.

QUESTION: Should Davon go to his boss and ask for a raise today?

☐ **a.** Yes. The boss will be pleased with his success and he has a good chance of getting a raise.

☐ **b.** He should go to his boss to share the good news. He can then ask for an appointment to review his salary.

☐ **c.** No, he shouldn't ask for a raise. He should wait until his boss calls him in for the regular salary review period.

4. SITUATION: Maria wants to take a computer course where she will learn how to publish an e-newsletter. It won't help her directly with her job but it will help in her volunteer position with a local charity. Unfortunately, the course begins at 5:00 p.m., an hour before Maria can leave the office. She's thinking of going to her manager, Michael, to ask about leaving early once a week – but she doesn't think he will allow it.

QUESTION: How can Maria best approach Michael? List at least two tips. The tips you learned in this book will give you some ideas.

1._____

_____

_____

_____

2._____

_____

_____

_____

_____

UNIT 9. ASSERTIVENESS

Assertive behavior means standing up for your rights and point of view.

In the real world, answers for the questions in this unit may vary. They depend on company culture, individual personality, and general business etiquette.

ANSWERS:
4 points for 1c, 2a, 2c, 3b
2 points for 3c and **1 point** for 3a.
For Question #4, score yourself. See page 186-187.

☐   ←   ←   ← WRITE YOUR SCORE HERE.

1. a [0 points]: *"Ladies first."* By now you should know that the business environment is supposed to be gender-neutral, so this sentence is not appropriate for a man to say in a meeting. Other reasons why this answer isn't the best:
- Marc might never have a chance to return to his original ideas.
- It encourages the interrupter to continue her bad habit by allowing her to be successful.
- Marc will seem timid, not assertive. Seeing this behavior, the Manager probably won't put him on the track to leadership roles.

Cultural note: Speaking up

Research shows that speaking habits are actually not entirely gender-neutral: The person who allows interruptions is more often a woman than a man. Girls are often taught not to be aggressive or even assertive but instead be nice, helpful and kind. They may take those lessons into their work lives.

INTERRUPTIONS

1. b [0 points]: **Keep talking**, talking louder than the interrupter. This kind of aggressive behavior can be seen in political talk shows on American television. However, it isn't typical in real business meetings. In fact, both people in this case are rude: the person who interrupts as well as the one who keeps talking.

1. c [**4 points**]: Say *"Excuse me, if I could just finish..."* It is OK to ask to continue speaking. This comment isn't rude if Marc says it politely. In fact, it shows that he knows how to defend himself fairly.

1. d [0 points]: *"please be quiet."* Even saying *please* is not enough: this order is aggressive and impolite for any business situation. As well, anything said with anger, or shouted, is not acceptable at work (emergencies excepted).

2. Company expectations about after-hours phone calls vary. Find out what your boss expects. A good boss will discuss this and also listen to your point of view.

2. a [**4 points**]: Depending on the company culture, it may be necessary to **give your full attention to your boss** whenever he/she calls, even when you're at home. This is especially true for employees who want to be promoted within the company.

ASKING YOUR BOSS FOR AN APPOINTMENT

2. b [0 points]: **Don't try multitasking when you talk** with your boss. Show respect for every caller by giving them your full attention. Never eat while you talk with someone on the phone; that is rude. Most phones, even cell phones, have good microphones and can transmit even quiet background noises.

2. c [**4 points**]: It depends on the company culture: In many cases, **it can be OK to ask your boss if you can call back.** This solution isn't rude if you follow good etiquette:
- ask, don't tell or order, the boss
- give a reason
- suggest a time to call back or ask your boss for a good time

2. d [0 points]: To say *"Now isn't a good time. I'm eating dinner with my family."* isn't very respectful to your boss (even if it's true). To be polite, see **c** above.

3. a [1 point]: It's not best to **ask for an immediate decision** on a raise. While this is assertive behavior, it is probably not wise because the boss needs some time to consider Davon's total contributions to the team. See all of **b** below.

3. b [4 points]: **Davon should ask for an appointment.** In some companies, especially in Sales Departments, raises aren't automatic, so it is then the responsibility of the employee as well as the manager to consider when a raise or promotion is appropriate. In that case it's OK for Davon to start the process.

BE PREPARED WHEN YOU MEET WITH YOUR BOSS

3. b (continued): Davon also needs time to think about a meeting. Although he has just had a good experience, he might be forgetting some less impressive days at work! A salary increase depends on a good track record, more than one success. In addition to successfully attracting new customers, sales employees need to have good soft skills.

3. c [2 points]: Getting contracts is his job. Davon can make notes of his successes during the year. If his company gives raises only once a year, he should make sure they are mentioned in the annual performance review (see box below).

Job Tip: A raise depends on a good track record, that means more than one success. Employees need to do superior work and demonstrate good soft skills, such as being helpful team members and communicating efficiently with coworkers, managers and clients. It's a good idea to keep track of all your recent achievements and professional development. Have the value of your contributions ready to present and discuss at a salary review. Your personal needs, for example caring for a growing family, are not a reason for an employer to give you a raise.

It is essential to know your market value, based on comparative salaries elsewhere, if possible. For example, consult payscale.com or glassdoor.ca. Decide before your meeting how much money you are asking for. (By the way, the more a person already earns, the more likely they are to get that raise when they ask for it!)[77]

Where regular annual reviews aren't the custom, an employee can request one. Note: in a unionized workplace, salaries are usually set and raises may be automatic.

NEGOTIATING STRATEGIES

4. Give yourself a point for any of the following **5 factors for Maria to consider** – up to a total of **4 points:**

#1. Time of day:
- **Morning** is **not** the best time. 8:00-11:00 a.m. is peak meeting time, according to productivity studies.[78]
- Managers often have less available time mornings than afternoons. As well, according to health experts, men are generally most competitive and aggressive in the morning.[79] So if Michael doesn't like Maria's request, they might not have an easy discussion then.
- Many people are a little more relaxed right **after lunch.** In the **afternoon** men are generally more open to discussion, "more agreeable to suggestion, less aggressive and defensive."[80] So the afternoon may be the best time to discuss a conflict.

In any case, Maria should choose:
- an appointment time that gives both people time to prepare their thoughts beforehand
- a time of day or week that is generally less stressful

Other factors besides time are important:

#2. Maria should consider beforehand what difficulties her request could cause Michael. Then she should **propose a solution to each difficulty.** After all, Maria is supposed to support her manager, not make him more trouble. For example, she should think about a replacement for herself when she leaves work early, as well as propose how she will make up the missing time, perhaps by coming in early or staying late.

SOFT SKILLS FOR NEGOTIATIONS

#3. Maria also needs to be respectful of Michael's ideas about her suggested solutions, since he is her boss.

#4. She should try to **find a benefit to Michael** and the company, some way that the training can help them. For example, she might be able to assist with a company newsletter after the training.

#5. Maria doesn't have a right to this unscheduled time off, so she should go into the talk with a **positive, co-operative attitude, using all her soft negotiation skills** (review Unit 8 HOW TO SAY IT).

This man has an aggressive, not assertive, posture. What aspects of his body language show aggression?

♦

Now go to page 194 and enter your scores for Part 3 in the chart. Add them up, then read about your soft skills for working with the boss. Now, of course, you know a lot more!

HOW TO SAY IT: INTERRUPTIONS AND AVOIDING INTERRUPTIONS

During an office discussion or conversation, you might want to join in with a comment, exclamation or objection to a particular point. That might mean interrupting someone. (Research shows that some men tend to dominate business discussions, and they interrupt women more often than the reverse.81) But it is possible to interrupt politely.

Here are some strategies for a polite interruption:

- **Body language**: get eye contact with the speaker and show through body language, for example a raised finger, that you want to say something.

- **One-syllable repetitions**: Say "*Umm...umm...*" or "*But...But...But...*" slowly until the speaker lets you talk. This strategy is best for informal discussions.

- **Ask to speak:**
  o "*May I just add something?...*"
  o "*Excuse me, I just want to say...*"
  o "*If I could just make one point here...*"
  o "*Could I just butt in for a moment?*" [informal]
  Notice the polite language, for example *may* and *could*, and the use of *just* to signal that you need only a very short time.

- **Start talking when the speaker pauses**, for example at the end of a sentence. That is generally considered a fair discussion practice.

On the other hand, when you are speaking, there will be times when you don't want interruptions. **Here are some strategies for preventing interruptions:**

- If you know at the start that you have several points to make:
  - o Tell the group how many points you want to make. While you explain your points, number them: *"First,...Second..., Third,... And last,..."* Then everyone will hear how your speech progresses and they will know when they can speak up.
  - o Say you'll answer questions at the end of your argument. (This is often done in presentations.)

  Although this strategy might not stop all interruptions, it is effective in most cases. Since you have made your plans clear, it would be a little rude for anyone to interrupt before you finish.

- Say you want (or ask) to finish your point:
  - o *"Excuse me, if I could just finish..."*
  - o *"If you can wait just a second, I'll finish up."*
  - o *"Just one more thing..."*
  - o *"May I just finish?"* (This isn't really a question.)
  Then **don't pause** for a response from the interrupter.

  These comments aren't rude if said in a friendly tone of voice. Notice again the polite language, using *Excuse me, If, Just* and *May* to start.

These are some polite, assertive strategies that show that you know how to defend yourself fairly.

ACTION:

What practical advice did you learn from this book about working with your colleagues and boss and getting ahead in your career? Review the book and make a list of tips that are important to you. (Writing a list helps you to remember.)

_____

_____

_____

_____

_____

_____

_____

_____

Hope you enjoyed finding out the unwritten rules of office communication! You're on track for success.

YOUR QUIZ SCORE AND WHAT IT MEANS

Read and use these scoring charts after you have finished the relevant units.

Part 1: Soft skills for making a good first impression

Enter your scores for each of the quizzes below and add them together:

Unit 1 _____ (p. 10)

Unit 2 _____ (p. 30)

Unit 3 _____ (p. 51)

Total = _____

There are 48 points in these three units. If you scored...

41 or more in total...
Very good! You know as much as most of your U.S. and Canadian colleagues about etiquette and soft skills in business greetings and first meetings, telephoning and email customs. You know where and how to answer your phone. And you have a good sense of the right level of formality to use with customers/clients and coworkers – in personal introductions, on the phone and in your email.

30-40 in total...
Good – You now have a good foundation in communication etiquette to build on. When you meet someone or get phone calls and email now, make a note of the greetings, closings and politeness of effective messages. You will quickly increase your business vocabulary and

sense of formality, because now you know what to notice. Review these chapters again until you feel confident about making introductions, telephoning and emailing in business contexts.

29 or less in total...
When you started this book, you were not yet familiar with some important soft skills for communication etiquette. Try to observe office workers' soft skills and language: how formally to do they speak in introductions? where and when do they use their phones? how formal/informal are their emails? Make notes on the vocabulary of effective messages that you receive. These chapters will guide you in choosing polite expressions. As you review them, you will become more comfortable with the English and etiquette of office communication. Practice speaking, listening, and writing in business situations as much as you can. You may make a few mistakes at first, but you will learn fast, because now you know what to be careful about.

Part 2: Soft skills for getting along in the office

Enter your scores for each of the quizzes below and add them together:

Unit 4 _____ (p. 74)

Unit 5 _____ (p. 98)

Unit 6 _____ (p. 120)

Total = _____

There are 48 points in Part 2. If you scored...

41 or more in total...
Very good! You have good communication and soft skills. You have a good sense of what coworkers like and dislike in the office and you are aware of social customs at work, such as attending or declining company events and socializing with coworkers. Probably your colleagues consider you to be quite likeable. Generally, you know the right level of politeness to use in different situations; and your participation in meetings and committee work is both supportive and confident.

30-40 in total...
You now have a good foundation in communication and soft skills to build on. If you scored much lower on Unit 4 than Unit 6, it probably means that you are a good worker but need to be a little more sensitive about your coworkers' likes and dislikes in the office and at company events. Remember that business isn't done only at meetings – small talk and social events are important for good working relationships. If you scored lower on Unit 6, it may mean that you enjoy socializing with coworkers more than asserting yourself at meetings. That is probably not the impression you want to give your boss and team leader, so review Unit 6. It will remind you about good meeting and teamwork skills.

29 or less in total...
When you started this book, you were not yet aware of some important soft skills for getting along with office colleagues. These units can guide you in choosing polite expressions for socializing and working with others. It would also be a good idea to observe peoples' soft skills

and language at work (but not on TV or in movies – such roles are often not typical!): how formal/informal are they with each other? how do they show that they want to get along and be supportive? Try to observe the behavior and vocabulary of successful meeting participants. As your awareness expands, you will become more comfortable with the spoken and unspoken language of office communication. Review these units and practice listening, speaking and learning in business situations as much as you can.

Part 3: Soft skills and assertiveness for working with the boss

Enter your scores for each of the quizzes below and add them together:

Unit 7 _____ (p. 140)

Unit 8 _____ (p. 162)

Unit 9 _____ (p. 182)

Total =   _____

There are 48 points in these three units. If you scored...

41 or more in total...
Congratulations! Your great communication and soft skills will help you to get along and get ahead. You usually know how to work with your boss and when not to bother him/her with questions. You are good at supporting him/her and don't play the "blame game." When you have a request, you support it with facts and solutions. In general, you are a good listener, give constructive feedback and contribute positively to the company. And when you reach the next level, others will be glad you are their manager.

30-40 in total...
You have generally good soft skills that are the basis for a positive working relationship with your boss. On some occasions you might not take enough initiative; or you might not be quite assertive enough, blaming yourself a little too much. Or perhaps you sometimes ask questions, react to feedback, or blame someone else too quickly, without considering the other person's point of view. But you usually understand managers correctly and respond appropriately. Look through the units and review questions that were difficult to answer. Note the suggested communication solutions and practice them whenever there is an opportunity.

29 or less in total...
When you started these units, you were not yet aware of some important soft skills for working with bosses and managers. With *Office Soft Skills* you have begun to develop critical communication patterns that can help your chances of getting ahead. You probably need to

pay more attention to the boss' words and tone of voice to make sure you understand whether a comment is a friendly reminder, a polite order, or asarcastic remark. In fact, listen carefully to your own voice as well: how do your comments sound to others? how have you responded to feedback from the boss? These issues are important for getting ahead. With expanded communication and soft skills, you will make progress now that you know what to be careful about.

REFERENCES

1. "Exploring the Handshake in Employment Interviews," Greg L. Stewart, Susan L. Dustin, Murray R. Barrick, Todd C. Darnold, *Journal of Applied Psychology*, vol. 93, 2008, pp.1139-1146.

2. "Exploring the Handshake in Employment Interviews," Greg L. Stewart et al., see #1 above.

3. "Competent Jerks, Lovable Fools, and the Formation of Social Networks," by Tiziana Casciaro and Miguel Sousa Lobo, *Harvard Business Review*, Vol. 83, No. 6, June 2005. Long abstract at: http://hbswk.hbs.edu/cgi-bin/print?id=4916

4. A Canadian poll on "Scents and sensibility," by Wallace Immen, *The Globe and Mail*, 23 August 2012, p. 2. @ https://www.theglobeanmail.com/report-on-business/scents-and-sensibility/article4314981/?page=1

5. "Face it, the 'beauty premium' exists at work," by Leah Eichler, *The Globe and Mail*, 11 January 2014, p. B15. @ https://www.theglobeandmail.com/report-on-business/careers/career-advice/life-at-work/lets-face-it-the-beauty-premium-exists-at-work/article16279790/

6. According to the men's fashion industry, since 2000 the number of men wearing ties has decreased approximately from 20 to 5 percent in "Tie's power slips," by staff at *Toronto Star*, 13 June 2008, p. L2.

7. Data from *Canadian HR Reporter* and TheLadders.com are referenced in "Power Points: On office etiquette" by Harvey Schachter, *The Globe and Mail*, 7 July 2008, p. B7. @ https://www.theglobeandmail.com/report-on-business/careers/management/power-points/article1341910/

8. Data on executives' preferences are from a survey by OfficeTeam in 2007, cited in "E-mail inbox flagged for its importance," by Virginia Galt, *The Globe and Mail*, 14 Dec. 2007, p. C3. @ https://www.theglobeandmail.com/report-on-business/e-mail-inbox-flagged-for-its-importance/article18151115/

9. "Less tech, more facetime," Backbonemag.com, Jun/Jul 2012, p.8.

10. "Nearly 50 per cent say phone is on hand 24/7: poll," byMichael Oliveira, Canadian Press, in *Toronto Star,* 28 Dec. 2013, @ https://www.thestar.com/business/tech_news/2013/12/27/nearly_50_ per_cent_say_phone_is_on_hand_247_poll.html

11. "Take a Break" by Larry Rosen, *Harvard Business Review,* June 2015. @ https://hbr.org/2015/06/conquering-digital-distraction? cm_ sp=Magazine%20Archive-_-Links-_-Previous%20Issues

12. "Nearly 50 per cent say phone is on hand 24/7: poll," by Michael Oliveira, 2013 – see #10.

13. Research done at universities in Scotland is cited in "No e-mails, please. I'm trying to work," by Rebecca Dube, *The Globe and Mail,* 18 Feb. 2008, pp. L1-L2.@ www.theglobeandmail.com/ life/no-e-mails-please-im-trying-to-work/article18445345/

14. (p. 37) "No e-mails, please. I'm trying to work," by Rebecca Dube – see #13.

15. (p. 37) "Information overload" was named the 'problem of the year' for 2008, according to Basex: "Is Information Overload a $650 Billion Drag on the Economy?" by Steve Lohr, *New York Times* on-line, 20 Dec. 2007. @ http://bits.blogs.nytimes.com/2007/12/20/ is-information-overload-a-650-billion-drag-on-the-economy/? ref=technology

16. "Why Is It So Hard to Do My Work?" by Sophie Leroy, in *Organizational Behavior and Human Decision Processes,* Vol. 109, #2 Jul 2009, pp 168-181. https://doi.org/10.1016/j.obhdp.2009.04.002

17. *Recruiting, Retaining, and Promoting Culturally Different Employees,* by Lionel Laroche and Don Rutherford, Elsevier, 2007, pp. 210, 215.

18. *Email Statistics Report, 2015-2019* by THE RADICATI GROUP, INC. (California, U.S.A.), Feb. 2015 @ http://www.radicati. com/wp/wp-content/uploads/2015/02/Email-Statistics-Report-2015-2019-Executive-Summary.pdf

19. "No e-mails, please. I'm trying to work," by Rebecca Dube – see #13.

20. "Virtual mail creates real time headache" by Bill Hendrick, Cox News Service, cited in the *Toronto Star*, 13 November, 2007, p. B8.

21. "No e-mails, please. I'm trying to work," by Rebecca Dube – see #13.

22. • U.S.A.: "Goofing off on the Internet at work may be masking rising productivity," by Bloomberg View columnist Noah Smith, 23 May 2017.@ www.theglobeandmail.com/report-on-business/rob-commentary/goofing-off-on-the-internet-at-work-may-be-masking-rising-productivity/article35090478/
   • U.K.: "The three-hour work day," by Andrew Ryan. *The Globe and Mail*, 21 Nov. 2013 @ www.theglobeandmail.com/life/facts-and-arguments/talking-points-three-hour-work-day-social-media-and-online-shopping-and-how-men-measure-up/article15530700/
   • Toronto, Canada: "Why Facebook is a good thing," by Paul Lima, *Technology Quarterly*, Winter 2007, p. 5.

23. "Tuned out: TV at your desk," by Craig Silverman, *The Globe and Mail*, 25 Feb. 2008, p. L3. @ https://www.theglobeandmail.com/ life/ reference-from-hell-i-would-not-touch-him/article718392/

24. "2013 year in review," *The Globe and Mail*, 28 Dec. 2013, p. F8.

25. "Canadians love to surf while they work," by Judy Gerstel, *Toronto Star*, 19 Nov. 2007 @ https://www.thestar.com/life/2007/11/19/canadians_love_to_surf_while_at_work.html

26. • "Sending personal e-mails: false sense of security," by Wallace Immen, *The Globe and Mail*, 5 July 2008, p. B21. @ https://www.theglobeandmail.com/report-on-business/sending-personal-e-mails-false-sense-of-security/article4220983/

27. "If it says NSFW, it really is not safe for work" by Craig Silverman, *The Globe and Mail*, 18 June 2007, p. L3.

@ https://www.theglobeandmail.com/life/if-it-says-nsfw-it-really-is-not-safe-for-work/article723764/

28. "Preparing new entrants for subordinate reporting," by Priscilla S. Rogers, Mian Lian Ho, Jane Thomas, Irene F. H. Wong and Catherine Ooi Lan Cheng, *Journal of Business Communication*, 41 (4), October 2004, p. 372. These authors cite K. O. Locker, *Business and Administrative Communication* (5th ed.), Irwin, 2000, p. 5.

29. "Canoodling coworkers: Sign on the dotted line" by Craig Silverman, *The Globe and Mail* online, 30 Mar. 2009.

30. "Let's register, Love," by Michael Kesterton in his col-umn "Social Studies," *The Globe and Mail*, 16 January 2008, p. L6.

31. The research by Essex University is cited in "Popular and Rich," by Michael Kesterton in his column "Social Studies," *The Globe and Mail*, 5 March 2009, p. L6.

32. Some of the advice is adapted from an article by diversity trainers Cynthia Reyes and Hamlin Grange: "Watch your language at work," *The Globe and Mail*, 10 March 2006.

33. "The rise of the do-gooder," by Daphne Gordon, *Toronto Star*, 13 March 2008, p. L3 @ http://www.thestar.com/ living/article /342593--the-rise-of-the-do-gooder.

34. A survey of 2,200 employees by the online job site TrueCareers is cited in "Watercooler," by Associated Press (e.g. as seen in *The Toronto Star*, p. D11), 10 Sept. 2005.

35. "Is it time to close the door on the open office?" by Brenda Bouw, *The Globe and Mail*, 22 March 2017. @ https://www.theglobeandmail. com/ report-on-business/careers/management/is-it-time-to-close-the-door-on-the-open-office/article34365896/

36. "Watercooler" – See #34 above.

37. "Watercooler" – See #34 above.

38. "Top 5 Workplace Etiquette Breaches in an Open Office Space" by Abby Welch, 5 Aug. 2014, refers to a poll among accounting and finance personnel. @ http://blog.accountemps.com/top-5-workplace-etiquette-breaches-in-an-open-office-space?utm_campaign=Hearsay&utm_medium=Link&utm_source=Hearsay

39. *We Know What You're Thinking* by Darrell Bricker and John Wright, of Ipsos Reid, Harper Collins, 2009, p. 24.

40. "Almost 40 per cent of Canadians eat lunch at their desks: study," by Lia Levesque, The Canadian Press, 18 May 2017. As seen @ http://www.theglobeandmail.com/life/health-and-fitness/health/almost-40-per-cent-of-canadians-eat-lunch-at-their-desks-study/article35045939/

41. *Recruiting, Retaining and Promoting Culturally Different Employees*, by Lionel Laroche and Dan Rutherford, Elsevier, 2007, p. 217.

42. "Can tuning in turn up productivity?" by Kira Vermond, *The Globe and Mail*, 27 September 2008, p. B21. @ https://www.theglobeandmail.com/report-on-business/can-tuning-in-turn-up-productivity/article4300466/

43. One such survey is: "The weekly web poll" – an online survey answered by 5,490 people – *The Globe and Mail*, 26 November 2004, p. C1.

44. *Report on Business*, April 2016, p. 13: Non-unionized workers stay home 7.5 days and union workers 13.2 days per year.

45. (p. 102) "Culture plays big role in absenteeism, study finds," by Bertrand Marotte, *The Globe and Mail*, 10 Oct. 2013 @ https://www.theglobeandmail.com/report-on-business/careers/career-advice/life-at-work/culture-plays-big-role-in-time-off-study-says/article14811329/#dashboard/follows/

46. A survey of 1,149 Americans is cited in "Sick or distracted, workers still show up," by Terry Brodie, *The Globe and Mail*, 19 September 2008. @ https://www.theglobeandmail.com/report-on-business/sick-or-distracted-workers-still-show-up/article659852/

47. Question 3 is adapted from Amy Verner's article "Overdressers: Beware of suspicious minds," *The Globe and Mail*, 14 July 2008, p. L1.@ www.theglobeandmail.com/life/overdressers-beware-of-suspicious-minds/article1057409/

48. *We Know What You're Thinking* by Darrell Bricker and John Wright, of Ipsos Reid, Harper Collins, 2009, p. 26.

49. "Is it appropriate for men to wear sandals to work during the summer?" *Toronto Star* Web Forum, 2 August 2007, p. AA8 (print edition); online abstract at: http://pqasb.pqarchiver.com/thestar/doc/439283344.html

50. "Teacher, you should lose some weight," by Noel Houck and John Fujimori, pp. 91, 95. In: *Pragmatics: Teaching Speech Acts*, D.H. Tatsuki & N. R. Houck, eds., TESOL, 2010, pp. 89-103.

51. *Looking Out/Looking In*, 2nd Canadian ed., by Ronald B. Adler, Neil Towne & Judith A. Rolls, Thomson/Nelson, 2004, p.52.

52. Centre for Canadian Language Benchmarks "Enhanced Language Training Research Report: What's Already Out There?" October 2004, p. 76. @ http://www.language.ca/index.cfm?Voir=sections&Id=17310&M=4037&Repertoire_No=2137991327

53. "internTIP of the Week" by Career Edge, 3April 2017.@http://campaign.r20.constantcontact.com/render?m=1106246343320&ca=9149b528-e437-4c3b-b6c1-b85e20a97fb6

54. Development Dimensions International, Inc. and Monster.com did a world-wide survey of more than 1,800 hirers. Cited in "No love lost here," by Virginia Galt, The Globe and Mail, 13 February 2008, p. C2. @ www.theglobeandmail.com/report-on-business/no-love-lost-here/article1351208/

55. *Work With Me: The 8 Blind Spots Between Men and Women in Business,* by Barbara Annis and John Gray, Palgrave Macmillan, 2013, p. 177.

56. A poll of 300 managers conducted by Robert Half Management Resources is cited in: http://www.hrreporter.com/article/23109-checking-email-in-meetings-frequent-occurrence-but-managers-dont-like-it-survey/#sthash.zGbiw0ZN.dpuf . 16 Dec. 2014

57. Background information for this question in: *Recruiting, Retaining, and Promoting Culturally Different Employees*, by Lionel Laroche and Don Rutherford, Elsevier, 2007, pp. 129-132.

58. *Managing Diversity: People Skills for a Multicultural Workplace*, 7th ed., by Norma Carr-Ruffino, Ph.D., Pearson Custom Publishing, 2006, p. 29.

59. "'Tis the season to be inundated," by David Aston, *The Globe and Mail*, 14 November 2007, p. C1. @ https://www.theglobeandmail.com/report-on-business/tis-the-season-to-be-inundated/article697693/

60. "The rise of the do-gooder," by Daphne Gordon, *Toronto Star*, 13 March 2008, p. L3 @ http://thestar.com/living/article/342593--the-rise-of-the-do-gooder.

61. "The most frequently used spoken American English idioms: A corpus analysis and its implications," by Dilin Liu, *TESOL Quarterly* Vol. 37 No.4, Winter 2003, 671-700.

62. Source of survey information for #2: CareerBuilder.com, cited in "Punctuality problems," metro (Toronto edition), 2 May 2006, p. 16.

63. "Growth in the 'gig economy' fuels work force anxieties," by Noam Scheiber, 12 July 2015, *New York Times* online @ www.nytimes.com/2015/07/13/business/rising-economic-insecurity-tied-to-decades-long-trend-in-employment-practices.html

64. "Trains, planes and conflicting values" by bizethics, *The Globe and Mail*, 17 October 2007, p. C6.

65. "Companies scaling down holiday parties," by Wallace Immen, The Globe and Mail, 23 Nov. 2011, p. B20 @ http://www.theglobeandmail.com/report-on-business/careers/career-advice/on-

the-job/companies-scaling-down-holiday-parties/article2245301/

66. These two quotations were published in *Recruiting, Retaining, and Promoting Culturally Different Employees*, by Lionel Laroche and Don Rutherford, copyright Elsevier (2007), pp. 201-203. Used with permission of the publisher.

67. Susan B. Butler, author of Become the CEO of You, Inc., as reported in "Being selfish can boost your career," by Leah Eichler, *The Globe and Mail*, 8 June 2012, p. B16 @ https://www.theglobeandmail. com/report-on-business/careers/career-advice/life-at-work/being-selfish-can-boost-your-career/article4242392/

68. A survey of 5,247 hiring managers by the U.S. consulting company Leadership IQ is cited in "Why new hires bomb: beyond technical skills," by Virginia Galt, *The Globe and Mail*, 21 Sept. 2005. @ www.theglobeandmail.com/report-on-business/why-new-hires-bomb-beyond-technical-skills/article986877/

69. "Preparing new entrants for subordinate reporting," by Priscilla S. Rogers, Mian Lian Ho, Jane Thomas, Irene F. Wong and Catherine Ooi Lan Cheng, *Journal of Business Communication* 41 (4), October 2004, especially pp. 391-392. Question #4 is based partly on items from their vocabulary lists.

70. Stephanie Whittaker cites Careerbuilder.com in her article "Lies, damned lies, and the workplace," *The Globe and Mail*, 7 March 2008, p. C1. @ https://www.theglobeandmail.com/report-on-business/lies-damned-lies-and-the-workplace/article668500/

71. "Lies, damned lies, and the workplace," by Stephanie Whittaker – see #70.

72. This has been commented on by several business writers, for example, "Ways women can hold their own in a male world," by Dana Mattioli, *Wall Street Journal*, WSJ.com, 25 Nov. 2008, @ http://online. wsj.com/article/SB122756745919254459.html

73. Beverly Kaye and Sharon Jordan-Evans, in Love'Em or Lose'Em: Getting Good People to Stay (Berrett-Koehler, 2009) and their website http://www.keepem.com. Some data here are based on their early

results, cited in "How bad does a boss have to be before employees bolt?" by Wallace Immen, *The Globe and Mail*, 29 June 2005, p. C3.

74. Two articles about angry women and men are:
"Angry women don't get ahead," by Claudia Parsons, Reuters News Agency (e.g., as appeared in *The Globe and Mail*, p. B17), 4 August 2007 "Repenting post-rant pays off for women," by Patrick White, *The Globe and Mail*, 7 April 2008, @ www.theglobeandmail.com/ life/ repenting-post-rant-pays-off-for-women/article18447939/

75. "Ways women can hold their own in a male world," by Dana Mattioli, *Wall Street Journal*, wsj.com, 25 November 2008. @ http:// online.wsj/article/SB122756745919254459.html

76. The advice here and in the paragraph "After the meeting" is adapted from wide readings, including the following:

• Patricia King, New York career consultant and author, in *Never Work for a Jerk* and *Monster Boss*.
• Dr. Bruce Katcher, president of the employee survey company Discovery Surveys Inc. in Massachusetts (U.S.A.), "Do you hate your boss?" online discussion with business reporter Virginia Galt, 20 August 2007 @ https://www. theglobeandmail.com/ opinion/do-you-hate-your-boss/article20400463/

77. "New study reveals the odds you'll actually get the raise you ask for," by Kerri Anne Renzulli, *Money* (online), 8 Jan. 2015. @ http:// time.com/money/3657524/odds-of-getting-raise/
78. In "Beat the clock: Choosing the best meeting time," Harvey Schachter explains studies by Mark Ellwood, Pace Productivity, Inc. *The Globe and Mail*, 13 Feb. 2012, p. B7 @ https://www. theglobeandmail.com/report-on-business/careers/beat-the-clock-choosing-the-best-meeting-time/article621208/

79. *Leadership and the Sexes: Using Gender Science to Create Success in Business*, by Michael Gurian with Barbara Annis, Jossey-Bass, 2008, p. 50.

80. *Leadership and the Sexes: Using Gender Science to Create Success in Business*, by Michael Gurian – see #79.

INDEX

Italicized page numbers refer to Questions.

OFFICE SOFT SKILLS: WORKING WITH NORTH AMERICANS

Manufactured by Amazon.ca
Bolton, ON

35308338R00120